JUBILEE

Published by IPC Magazines Limited,
King's Reach Tower,
Stamford Street, London, SE1 9LS
at the recommended price
shown on the frontispiece

Printed in England by Jarrold and Sons Limited,
Whitefriars, Norwich, NR3 1SH

ISBN 85037 364 6

£1·60

Managing Editor
Jane Reed

Editor
Douglas Keay

Art Editor
Keith Russell

Production Editors
Peter Watson, Editorial
Tony Skudder, Art

Picture Editor
Dennis Beaven

Picture Research
Brian Mumford
Percy Hatchman

Editorial Research
Marion Collins

Photographic Contributors

John Scott/Overseas and Feature Agency Ltd., and Marcus Adams; Associated Newspapers; Associated Press; Baron; Cecil Beaton; Camera Press; Central Press; Crown Copyright Reproduced by Permission of the Controller, HMSO; Daily Mirror; Fox Photos; Peter Grugeon; GPU; Anwar Hussein; Illustrated London News; Keystone; Patrick Lichfield; Mansell Collection; New Zealand Government; Norman Parkinson; Planet; Press Association; Radio Times; Scotsman; Lisa Sheridan; Snowdon; Spectrum; Times; Topical; UPI; Mark Westwood; Edward Wing; Woman's Own; Reproduced by gracious permission of Her Majesty the Queen

Contents

"We love Her as Queen, and we love her for herself"

Sir Winston Churchill, Coronation Day, June 2, 1953

The royal family tree

Prince Edward (1964–)

Prince Andrew (1960–)

Prince Charles (1948–)

Princess Anne (1950–)
m Capt. Mark Phillips

Queen Elizabeth II (1926–)
Reign 1952–
m Prince Philip, Duke of Edinburgh (1921–)

Edward, Duke of Kent (1935–
m Katharine Worsley

Princess Alexandra (1936–
m Hon. Angus Ogilvy

Richard, Duke of Gloucester (1944–)
m Birgitte van Deurs

Prince William (1941–1972)

Henry, Duke of Gloucester (1900–1974)
m Lady Alice Montagu-Douglas-Scott

Princess Margaret (1930–
m Antony Armstrong-Jones
Earl of Snowdon

King George VI (1895–1952)
Reigned 1936–1952
m Lady Elizabeth Bowes-Lyon (1900–)

Alice (1885–1969)
m
Prince Andrew of Greece

George, Duke of Kent (1902–1942)
m Princess Marina of Greece (1906–1968)

Prince Michael (1942–)

King Edward VIII (1894–1972)
Reigned Jan–Dec 1936
m Mrs. Wallis Warfield

Louise (1889–1965)
m King Gustav of Sweden

George, Marquess of Milford Haven (1892–1938)

George, Earl of Harewood (1923–)

Victoria Mary (1863–1950)
m Prince Louis of Battenberg
1st Marquess of Milford Haven

Mary, Princess Royal (1897–1965)
m 6th Earl of Harewood (1882–1947)

King George V (1865–1936)
Reigned 1910–1936
m Princess Mary of Teck (1867–1953)

Louis, Earl Mountbatten (1900–)
m Hon. Edwina Ashley

Hon. Gerald Lascelles (1924–)

Prince Arthur (1850–1942)

Prince Alfred (1844–1900)

King Edward VII (1841–1910)
Reigned 1901–1910
m Alexandra, Princess of Denmark (1844–1925)

Princess Alice (1843–1878)
m Grand Duke of Hesse (1837–1892)

Princess Helena (1846–1923)

Prince Leopold (1853–1884)

Princess Louise (1848–1939)

Queen Victoria (1819–1901)
Reigned 1837–1901
m Prince Albert of Saxe-Coburg-Gotha (1819–1861)

Princess Victoria (1840–1901)

Princess Beatrice (1857–1944)

DICK BARNARD

6

The Queen's Jubilee Year Diary

FEBRUARY
6 Accession Day
10 Leave London Airport for Eastern Samoa
11 Embark on Britannia for Western Samoa
14 Arrive Tonga
16 and 17 Fiji
22 to **March 7** Tour of New Zealand
MARCH
7 to 23 Tour of Australia
23 Leave Adelaide, Australia, by air for Port Moresby
23 to 26 Papua New Guinea
26 to 30 Australia, then return by air to London
MAY
4 Presentation of loyal addresses by both Houses of Parliament
5 Review of the united police forces of Britain
17 Glasgow Cathedral—a thanksgiving service
18 Cumbernauld and Stirling
19 Perth and Dundee
20 Aberdeen
23 Service for the Order of the Thistle at St. Giles Cathedral, Edinburgh
24 Opening of the General Assembly of the Church of Scotland in Edinburgh
26 Garden party at Holyroodhouse, Edinburgh
27 Opening of the new airport terminal, Edinburgh
JUNE
7 Thanksgiving service at St. Paul's Cathedral. Walk to lunch at the Guildhall. Broadcast to the Commonwealth

9 River Progress on the Thames; firework display
11 Trooping the Colour and RAF fly-past
13 Order of the Garter service at Windsor
20 Tour of the north-west—Lancashire, Merseyside and Greater Manchester
21 Embark on Britannia at Holyhead
22 Arrive at Gwynedd
23 Tour of West Wales and visit to Swansea
24 Tour of South Wales and visit to Cardiff
28 Review of the Royal Navy at Spithead, off Portsmouth
30 The first tour of London
JULY
6 Second London tour
7 Review of the British army in West Germany
11 Tour of Suffolk and Norfolk. Embark on Britannia
12 and 13 Tour of Humberside and Yorkshire
14 and 15 Tour of the north-east counties
19 Garden party at Buckingham Palace
21 Garden party at Buckingham Palace
26 Garden party at Buckingham Palace
27 Tour of the West Midlands
28 Tour of Derbyshire and Nottinghamshire
29 Review of the RAF at Finningley
AUGUST
4 Embark on Britannia at Southampton
5 Tour of Devon and inspection of Royal Marines at Plymouth
6 Tour of Cornwall
8 Tour of Avon
10 and 11 Tour of Northern Ireland
OCTOBER
Leave for tour of Canada

Right: *The Queen, wearing the Imperial State Crown— a picture taken for the State Opening of Parliament in November 1976*

Two delightful pictures of the Queen, taken at Balmoral specially to celebrate the Silver Jubilee

Death and accession

Princess Elizabeth was only 25 when her father died. She had been married for just over four years and she and her naval officer husband were enjoying bringing up their two small children, Charles and Anne. But now, with the sudden death of King George VI, Elizabeth was Queen.

Few people outside the Royal Family had known how ill the King was. In March 1949 he had undergone an operation to improve the circulation in his right foot. In 1951 it was confirmed he had a growth in his left lung but, after an operation, he seemed to have made such a good recovery that plans were organised for a holiday in South Africa the following March.

Princess Elizabeth and Prince Philip were due to leave on a tour of East Africa, Australia and New Zealand on the last day of January 1952 and, the night before they left, the King felt well enough to take his family to see South Pacific at London's Drury Lane.

But the following day was cold and bleak, with a biting wind, and people were shocked to see the newspaper pictures showing how gaunt and ill the King looked as he waved his daughter and son-in-law goodbye at London Airport.

Five days later King George was at Sandringham and enjoying a day's rough shooting, tramping over frost-crusted earth for nearly six hours. He came home to join the Queen and their grandchildren for tea in the nursery, and after dinner listened to the news on the wireless about Princess Elizabeth's tour. He retired to his bedroom on the ground floor about 10.30, read a magazine, and drank a cup of cocoa. At 7.30 the following morning one of his valets entered the room, drew back the curtains, and found that the King had died in his sleep. The cause was coronary thrombosis. His age was 56.

Prince Philip broke the news to his wife. They had spent the night in a small observation house, now called Treetops, in the Aberdare Forest of Kenya watching and filming wild life. By the following afternoon when a news agency report had been officially confirmed, they were back at the royal hunting lodge at Sagana, where they were spending a few days holiday.

Immediately, arrangements were made for the new Queen to fly to Entebbe, and then on through that night and the next day to London. Her plane landed at London Airport on an evening of drizzly darkness. As she came down the steps, in black and quite alone, her senior ministers of Government and Opposition—Winston Churchill and Clement Attlee—bowed, bare-headed, in grief and homage. It seemed, that night, as though the whole life of the nation were stilled, as in prayer. Almost 400 years after Elizabeth I, a second Elizabeth had acceded to the Throne of England, and under the sadness lay hope that a new, golden age might soon begin.

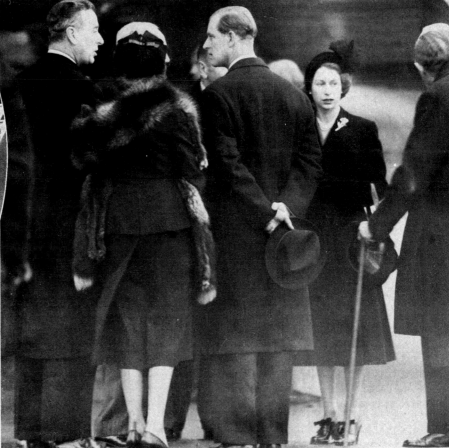

Left: *King George VI waves farewell to his daughter and Prince Philip as they set out from London Airport for Africa on January 31, 1952. Six nights later the King died in his sleep at Sandringham*

Above: *The new Queen arrives back in London after a night and day flight from Kenya. Awaiting her are Prime Minister Winston Churchill, Clement Attlee and Anthony Eden*

Above right: *A few minutes after leaving the aircraft, the Queen is surrounded by her relatives and ministers, yet already seems almost alone*

Right: *Queen Mary at the lying-in-state of her son, King George VI, with his widow, the Queen Mother, and his daughter, the new Queen Elizabeth*

Left: *The Queen's procession on the way to Westminster Abbey passes under Admiralty Arch, and (oval) the view a few moments earlier from the top of the Arch looking back up the Mall to Buckingham Palace*

Above: *The magnificent gold State Coach passes the Victoria Memorial as it leaves Buckingham Palace carrying the uncrowned Queen and Prince Philip. Standing at a second floor central window are Prince Charles and Princess Anne*

Below: *In the Mall at 5.30 a.m. where crowds of well-wishers have been camping out all night*

The Coronation

Sir Winston Churchill found the most apt way of describing how the people of Britain and the Commonwealth felt about the Coronation: "A day the oldest are proud to have lived to see and the youngest will remember all their lives."

June 2, 1953 was the actual day, but months were spent in preparation. The late Duke of Norfolk, the hereditary Earl Marshal, was in overall charge of the organisation, and Prince Philip was Chairman of the Coronation Commission. Among the many questions that had to be settled was whether or not the Prince should ride in the same coach as the Queen, or alongside on horseback. Queen Anne was the only other Queen to have had a consort at her coronation—and she had been carried to the Abbey in a chair because she suffered so badly from gout.

Should the service be televised? No, said the Coronation Commission. Yes, said the Queen. And when she studied the proposed route to and from Westminster Abbey she asked that it be extended so that more children would be able to see the procession.

The Imperial State Gown had to be remodelled for the Queen, a special mark was made on St. Edward's Crown to indicate the front—there had been a moment of uncertainty at the coronation of George VI—and the massive State Coach had to be completely refurbished.

In May, the decorations went up in the streets, and bunting was strung on stands along the procession route that was to accommodate 100,000 spectators. Ten thousand service-men—a quarter of them from overseas—were to march in the procession which would be so big it would take 45 minutes to pass any one position.

There would be five sections in the procession, starting out from different points. The first would be the Lord Mayor's procession, which would leave from the Mansion House at 8 a.m.—a good two hours before the Queen left the Palace. Next to start would be the colonial rulers, and after them the nine carriages of the Prime Ministers from the Commonwealth. Two thousand bandsmen, in 46 bands, would either be in the procession or stationed along the route, and 250 police horses would be specially trained for their Coronation Day duties . . .

As the facts and figures came tumbling out, the public began to grasp the scope of the occasion. In towns and villages, as well as in London itself, coronation committees (often the same people who had run the wartime Home Guard and WVS) organised their own celebrations and decorated the streets. At Hinton St. George, Somerset (population 350) they spent £10 on decorations, £13 on souvenir mugs for the village children, and £1. 15s. on souvenir spoons for the babies born between January 1 and June 2, 1953. Coronation Day itself was greeted by the church bell-ringers with a peal of Grandsire Doubles at 6.30 a.m., and three television sets were installed in the Victory Hut because only four people in the village had sets of their own.

In London, June 2 dawned cold and

13

Above: *Massive crowds of well-wishers, using every vantage point to ensure they had a good view, watched the procession to Westminster Abbey. It took over an hour to pass by them*

Below: *After the crowning ceremony, Prince Philip is the first to pay homage to the Queen*

Right: *The moment of crowning, as the Archbishop of Canterbury holds high St. Edward's Crown*

Oval: *Prince Charles poses a question to his grandmother as Princess Margaret looks on*

Bottom right: *Carrying the Sceptre with the Cross, and the Orb (symbol of the dominion of the Cross over the Sword) the Queen leaves the Abbey after her crowning*

drizzly, but thousands had camped out on the pavements all night, and even longer—73-year-old Zoe Neame took her place in Trafalgar Square 52 hours before the start of the procession. No-one minded whether they got soaked or not and those who had been there long enough saw *four* processions—to and from the Abbey on the day itself, and the rehearsal in early light the day before.

Tier upon tier of seats had been erected in Westminster Abbey for the 7,000 guests invited to the Coronation from all over the world. Each person was allocated 18 inches of space—except for peers of the realm, who, with their bulky ermine-edged cloaks, were permitted an extra inch.

At 10.20 a.m. the Queen set out from Buckingham Palace in the gold State Coach, drawn by eight Windsor greys, with four postillions in their dark velvet caps and gold braid jackets, red-coated footmen and Yeomen of the Guard. Seated with the Queen, who was dressed in a white silk gown embroidered with the emblems of the Commonwealth, was her Consort, Prince Philip, wearing the full dress uniform of an admiral of the fleet.

A fanfare of trumpets rang round the walls of the Abbey as Her Majesty entered, and, according to custom, the cry went up from the Westminster scholars: "Vivat Regina Elizabeth! Vivat! Vivat!"

Next came the recognition, a survival from Roman times when the Emperor was lifted up on a shield to be acclaimed by his soldiers. John Betjeman, now Sir John Betjeman, the Poet Laureate, was in the Abbey and this is how he described the scene at the time:

"First the Archbishop presents her to the clergy, who sit in the Sanctuary. Then to us in the South Transept, then to the people in the Nave, then to the East Transept, always with the same words: 'Sirs I here present unto you Queen Elizabeth, your undoubted Queen; Wherefore all you who are come this day to do your homage and service, are you willing to do the same?'. And each time we, her people, answer 'God save Queen Elizabeth,' and she makes a little curtsy. There is silence and trumpets sound."

The whole Coronation ceremony lasted several hours and there were one or two moments when the vast audience watching it on television wondered if the strain might prove too great for the young Queen. When the St. Edward's Crown—weighing all of five pounds—was gently placed upon her head, for a moment the Queen's shoulders sagged. The crowning is the dramatic climax of the service, when, at once, all the peers put on their coronets, the kings-of-arms their crowns, and the bishops their caps. And everyone stands, and all the people shout "God Save the Queen", and the trumpets sound, and the guns are fired at the Tower of London.

Somebody whose name was not printed in the order of ceremonial was the four-year-old Prince Charles, whose nanny dressed him in a cream silk blouse and trousers and, with his parents' approval, slipped him into the royal box during the service. He stood between the Queen Mother and Princess Margaret, his head just above the pew, busy much of the time asking his granny questions and burrowing in her handbag for a sweet.

The service ended shortly before 2 p.m. and the procession set out to return to the Palace, the first coaches leaving an hour before the Queen. To the deafening cheers

Above: *The Queen poses with members of the Royal Family after returning from Westminster Abbey*

Left: *Several hours after the Coronation ceremony, crowds were still thronging to the Palace gates*

Above right: *Watching the fly-past of the RAF from the balcony of Buckingham Palace*

Right: *The crowds were 12 deep at Hyde Park on the return journey from the Abbey, even though it had been raining much of the day*

of thousands—they leaned from every window, climbed every lamp-post, and waved a sea of Union Jacks—the crowned Queen returned home. The whole Royal Family then went on to the balcony to acknowledge the cheers and to take the salute of the RAF fly-past.

During the evening, with the streets still shining wet, 50,000 people pressed to the gates of the Palace, calling "We want the Queen", and time and again she and the Duke of Edinburgh stepped on to the balcony to wave back. In a broadcast that night the Queen said: "As this day draws to its close I know that my abiding memory of it will be, not only the solemnity and beauty of the ceremony, but the inspiration of your loyalty and affection."

The next day the Queen carried out an investiture, presented 2,400 Coronation medals, toured flag-bedecked streets in north London, and attended a state banquet in the evening before going out on to the balcony to acknowledge the cheers of the crowds who came in their thousands that night, and the night after that.

The Young Princess

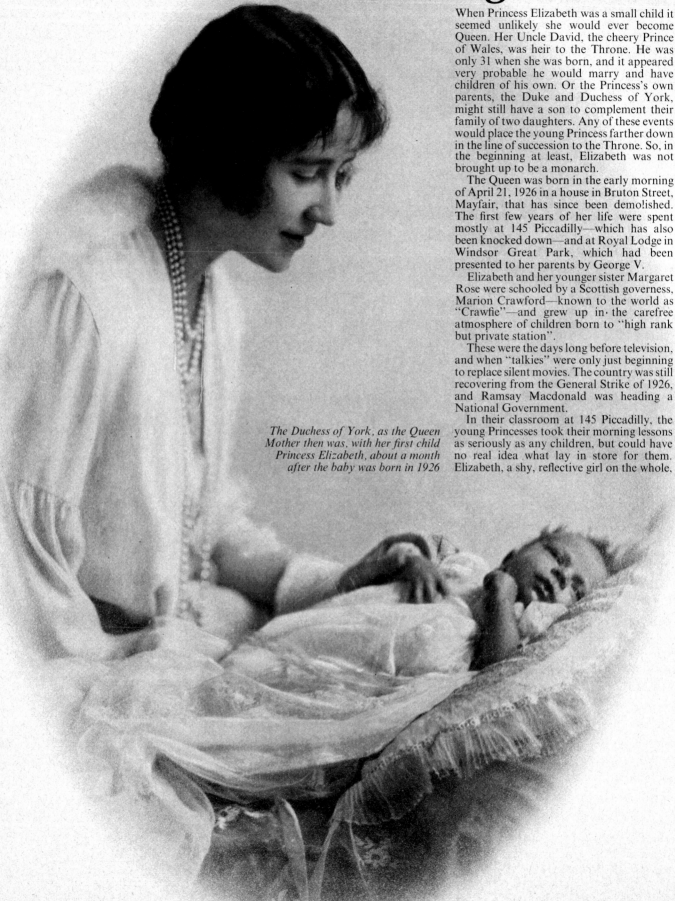

When Princess Elizabeth was a small child it seemed unlikely she would ever become Queen. Her Uncle David, the cheery Prince of Wales, was heir to the Throne. He was only 31 when she was born, and it appeared very probable he would marry and have children of his own. Or the Princess's own parents, the Duke and Duchess of York, might still have a son to complement their family of two daughters. Any of these events would place the young Princess farther down in the line of succession to the Throne. So, in the beginning at least, Elizabeth was not brought up to be a monarch.

The Queen was born in the early morning of April 21, 1926 in a house in Bruton Street, Mayfair, that has since been demolished. The first few years of her life were spent mostly at 145 Piccadilly—which has also been knocked down—and at Royal Lodge in Windsor Great Park, which had been presented to her parents by George V.

Elizabeth and her younger sister Margaret Rose were schooled by a Scottish governess, Marion Crawford—known to the world as "Crawfie"—and grew up in· the carefree atmosphere of children born to "high rank but private station".

These were the days long before television, and when "talkies" were only just beginning to replace silent movies. The country was still recovering from the General Strike of 1926, and Ramsay Macdonald was heading a National Government.

In their classroom at 145 Piccadilly, the young Princesses took their morning lessons as seriously as any children, but could have no real idea what lay in store for them. Elizabeth, a shy, reflective girl on the whole,

The Duchess of York, as the Queen Mother then was, with her first child Princess Elizabeth, about a month after the baby was born in 1926

was not terribly interested in geography, but excelled in French. She was inordinately proud of becoming a good swimmer. One day each week her grandmother, Queen Mary, took the Princess on "educational visits" to museums and art galleries so that she would grow up with a sense and knowledge of history—and perhaps because the Queen knew from personal experience how fate can completely alter a person's life. (Weeks before Queen Mary was to have married Edward VII's eldest son, the Duke of Clarence, her fiancé died. Subsequently she married the King's second son who became George V).

From a very early age, Princess Elizabeth loved the outdoor life. She particularly enjoyed the weekends she spent at Royal Lodge, Windsor, taking lessons in horse-riding. And the summer holidays with her parents at Birkhall, a few miles from Balmoral, where she first started to discover the moorland tracks and paths that she was to grow to love so well.

"Lilibet"—as she was known to the family—was adored by her grand-papa, George V, and when he died in 1936 the nine-year-old Princess may have sensed fully, for the first time, the responsibility of inheritance. Her uncle, Edward VIII, was now King but her father was next in line to the Throne.

Less than a year later Edward had abdicated in order to marry the woman he loved. In turn, George VI was crowned King and gradually, through her education and the caring attitude of those around her, it was borne in on the 10-year-old Elizabeth what her own position was one day to be.

Above right: *The two sisters, Princess Elizabeth and Princess Margaret Rose, in February 1939, a few months before the outbreak of World War II*
Below: *Princess Elizabeth at 2¼ years*
Right: *As a one-year-old, sitting in her pram*

Above: *The Queen's love of dogs—corgis in particular—was apparent from the time she was a small girl*

Left: *Princess Elizabeth accompanies King George V and Queen Mary to Westminster Abbey, in 1934*

Below left: *The whole family together, in 1936, at the Princesses' play-house at Royal Lodge, Windsor*

Below: *Princess Elizabeth plays Prince Charming to a Princess Margaret Cinderella in one of the wartime pantomimes at Windsor Castle*

Above: *As a young girl, out riding in the woods near Windsor*

Right and above right: *Queen Elizabeth and her family during the war years—around 1942—which was about the time that Prince Philip, on service with the Royal Navy, was visiting Windsor Castle during his shore leaves and making friends with Princess Elizabeth*

Below: *Princess Elizabeth changing a wheel during her wartime service with the ATS, the fore-runner of the Women's Royal Army Corps*

The royal line

According to respected genealogists the Queen can trace her ancestry back not only to King Harold, who fell at the Battle of Hastings 900 years ago, but also to George Washington, first President of the United States, and to Mutamid Ibn Abbad Cadi, King of Seville, whose reign began two years after William the Conqueror's. Indeed, only a few generations ago, the Queen's ancestors were also related to commoners with names such as George Smith and Mary Browne.

But nowadays Queen Victoria is generally as far back as most people go when thinking of the Queen's royal line of ancestors.

Victoria, who reigned longer than any other Queen—from 1837 to 1901—had nine children who married into several of the royal houses of Europe. One of her children, Princess Alice, married the Grand Duke Louis IV of Hesse in 1862, and their granddaughter married Prince Andrew of Greece, the father of the Duke of Edinburgh. So both the Queen and her husband are great-great-grandchildren of Queen Victoria, and are distant cousins to one another.

One of the interesting facts of royal lineage is that of the four monarchs before Elizabeth II, two were not born heirs apparent. Edward VII's eldest son, Prince Albert Victor, Duke of Clarence, died before coming to the Throne and his younger brother became George V. And George VI, the Queen's father, was not born to be King, but ascended the Throne after his brother David became Edward VIII then abdicated before he was actually crowned.

1. *An historic picture, taken nearly 80 years ago, of Queen Victoria and her family at Osborne House, Isle of Wight*

2. *Edward VII, on the right, with his eldest son, the Duke of Clarence—who died before coming to the Throne—on the left. Queen Alexandra is in the centre*

3. *A family group at the Duke of York's wedding in 1923. The Prince of Wales, later Edward VIII, is on the left*

4. *The 14-month-old Princess Elizabeth, on her mother's knee, and her father, her grandparents—King George V and Queen Mary—and the Earl and Countess of Strathmore*

5. *The home-coming of the Prince of Wales from a tour of India in 1922. On the right are Lord Lascelles and Princess Mary*

6. *King George VI and his family at Royal Lodge, Windsor, in 1942*

Secretary's Office requiring her authority the Sovereign, by tradition, always places her signature at the top.

Discussions with aides and officials usually occupy at least an hour, after which the Queen may go on to preside over a meeting of the Privy Council where, again by tradition, the whole of the business is carried out with everyone, including Her Majesty, remaining standing. Privy Council meetings take place less than twice a month, however, so it is more likely the Queen's day will continue with her receiving in audience perhaps a new ambassador to the Court of St. James, or a retiring judge, or a newly-appointed Cabinet Minister. If her meeting is with a high-ranking foreign visitor or someone she has known for a long time, it is quite possible that the Queen will invite her guest to stay on for lunch.

About nine times a year Her Majesty gives informal luncheon parties for between eight and 12 people, from a wide variety of backgrounds. A fairly typical guest list might include a bishop, a cricketer, an industrialist and a comedian. These lunches, one of the Queen's own innovations to help her meet a cross-section of interests, have proved a great success. But when they have no other engagements—and especially now that their children have grown up—the Queen and Prince Philip will lunch on their own, helping themselves from dishes on a hot-plate and very often parting company immediately after the meal.

Many afternoons the Queen and her husband have separate public engagements in or near London—though the Queen usually keeps Monday afternoons free for her hairdresser, after her return from the weekend at Windsor or Sandringham. Other afternoons are often occupied with dress fittings or sitting for a portrait.

In the comparatively rare event of there being no evening engagement, the Queen will sometimes spend an hour or so watching television. To no-one's surprise, she enjoys programmes to do with racing or show-jumping. She doesn't raise the ratings on high-brow plays or pop concerts, but she does like following the dramatised accounts of her forbears. The television drama series Edward VII was a particular favourite.

But all of this is only the pattern of the Queen's day when she is in London. A great deal of the year is spent in travelling, either on royal tours of Britain or more protracted visits to Commonwealth countries, when it is not unusual for the Queen's day to start at 7 a.m. and end at midnight.

Even when she is relaxing at Balmoral in the summer, or Sandringham in the New Year, she cannot escape work altogether. The despatch boxes are there every morning, awaiting the Queen's attention.

All in a Queen's day

The Queen is usually called at eight o'clock each morning, whether it's a working day or a holiday. The only exceptions are if she is ill or has a particularly early engagement.

After breakfast and going through the newspapers—with, perhaps, a start on the crosswords—she goes to her desk which, in Buckingham Palace, is in a study-cum-living room on the first floor. This room was once her mother's sitting-room.

On a table at the side of the desk lie the first of the day's despatch boxes. The pile of documents inside these boxes, or cases, are delivered to the Queen every day, either by train, plane, or helicopter, no matter which part of the world she happens to be in. They may include Cabinet papers, confidential Foreign Office reports and telegrams from heads of Commonwealth countries.

The Queen's Private Secretary is usually her first visitor of the day, bringing more papers to study and draft letters to be approved.

Contrary to what many people imagine, the Queen reads all letters addressed to her personally before passing them on for action. An interesting sidelight is that when it comes to documents from the Home

To commemorate...

Souvenirs come in three forms: the cheap, the nasty and the very expensive. And quite often it is the first and the second that survive and become period pieces—nothing stays nasty once it's become an antique!

The Victorians, with their love of bric-a-brac, enjoyed a bonanza. Their Queen reigned long enough to be celebrated in silver, golden and even diamond jubilee mugs, plates and trinkets.

George V's silver jubilee souvenirs, now 42 years old, are worth several times the money that was paid for them, as are the George VI coronation mugs that are prized possessions in many a family's china cupboard. (One particularly rare souvenir shows Prince Philip in the uniform of a naval commander—a rank he never held.)

But most people like to hold on to their commemorative plates, cups and saucers, with portraits of the monarch, as keep-sakes. At Queen Elizabeth's coronation, commemorative mugs were given to school-children and now their owners—in near to middle-age—can recall to their own children what the Coronation Day, June 2, 1953, meant to them.

For the present Silver Jubilee year nearly everything from a key-ring costing a few pence, to a commemorative plate in gold on sterling silver priced at nearly £400 is on sale to souvenir collectors. But there are rules for "approved" souvenirs, issued by the Lord Chamberlain at St. James's Palace, which emphasise that the item must be "in good taste" and free from any form of advertisement, and must carry no implication of royal custom or approval.

Prince Charles was chairman of a Design Centre panel that vetted over 250 products from over 90 companies. They found "surprisingly few manufacturers had taken advantage of this historic occasion to produce well designed modern products which would express to future generations the spirit of design in the 1970s". Maybe most people just prefer their souvenirs to look old-fashioned, even when they're new.

A selection of commemorative souvenirs including a jig-saw with two pieces missing, from King George V's Silver Jubilee in 1935, and a plate dating from as far back as Queen Victoria's Diamond Jubilee in 1897

Miniature thrones and crowns . . . brooches and medals . . . tin boxes and paper napkins . . . Almost anything can be made as a souvenir. There are few rules but for this Jubilee year a time was set—October—after which no more 1977 Jubilee souvenirs should be manufactured

The Queen's Mother

Nowadays Queen Elizabeth the Queen Mother is many people's idea of the perfect granny. Just as she seemed to be the perfect wife and Queen Consort for King George VI during his reign. She has the gift of always being regal while at the same time putting strangers immediately at their ease. And yet the strange part is that as a young woman she dreaded the idea of being in the public eye, even to the extent of turning down the Duke of York's offer of marriage in case he might one day be king.

Elizabeth Bowes-Lyon was born 77 years ago, the fourth daughter and ninth child of Lord and Lady Glamis. Her nurse found her "an exceptionally happy, easy baby; crawling early, running at 13 months and speaking very young". She was brought up partly at Glamis Castle, Angus, in Scotland, where, according to Shakespeare, Macbeth murdered King Duncan; and partly in a red brick Georgian house at St. Paul's Walden Bury in Hertfordshire. She grew up to be not only a beautiful girl, with summer-blue eyes and strong dark eyebrows, but a bewitching little person who, according to one London hostess, "was irresistible to men".

Lady Bowes-Lyon—her father had by now inherited the title of 14th Earl of Strathmore and Kinghorne—made her debut at Court in 1919, and the following year the 25-year-old Duke of York, second son of King George V, was invited twice to Glamis Castle. He wrote to his mother: "It is delightful here and Elizabeth is very kind to me. The more I see of her the more I like her."

Bertie, as he was known to his family, suffered badly from a stammer which made him dreadfully shy and at times depressed. In Elizabeth he found someone who sincerely wanted to help him, who believed his stutter *could* be cured. He fell very much in love with her, and she with him. But when he plucked up the courage to ask her to marry him, she reluctantly declined. "I think," wrote her mother later, "she was torn between her longing to make Bertie happy and her reluctance to take on the big responsibilities which this marriage must bring."

Almost three years later the King's son spent a weekend with Elizabeth and her family at their Hertfordshire home and, remembering George V's words—"You will be a lucky fellow if she accepts you"—he proposed once more. And this time he was lucky. Elizabeth had decided; she would marry and help the man she loved, even though she was aware she would never know real privacy again. (It is strange to reflect that, if she had realised at the time how much she would come to be loved by millions of people around the world, Elizabeth might have had less hesitation in accepting Bertie's first proposal.)

What she could never have guessed was

Through the years the Queen Mother has remained graciously beautiful. In the small picture (above left) she with her favourite brother, David the youngest of the Earl of Strathmore's ten children. And in the oval picture, right, we see her as a lovely girl of
Left: With the King and Winston Churchill, Queen Elizabeth, as she was then, inspects the bomb damage at Buckingham Palace, September

that her brother-in-law would abdicate the Throne in order to marry a twice-divorced American, and her own husband would become King at the age of 41, after 13 years of marriage. A gipsy palmist's prophesy, when she was seven, that she would one day become Queen did indeed come true.

The second world war broke out three years after King George VI's accession, and the people who had loved Elizabeth as a modern-thinking Duchess, giving such strength to her husband, saw another person: a Queen who refused to fly to safety in Canada with her children; who, always immaculately dressed, could bring fresh hope to blitz victims just by walking and talking with them in the rubble of their homes. As Winston Churchill said: "Many an aching heart has found some solace in her gracious smile." And as the Queen Mother herself said, after Buckingham Palace had been hit for the first of nine times: "I'm glad we've been bombed. It makes me feel I can look the East End in the face."

In common with many women of her age, the Queen Mother has not escaped personal tragedy. For years she watched her husband suffering from cancer. Her younger brother, David, who had been very close to her since childhood, died in 1961. And she, perhaps more than anyone, must have been saddened when her younger daughter and her husband decided to separate.

But there is much more that makes this very young old lady laugh and be happy. First, there are her six grandchildren. She is devoted to them, and they to her. There is her Castle of Mey in the far north of Scotland, and her house of Birkhall, near Balmoral. There is her fishing on the River Dee, and her love of antiques. There are her horses and her passion for horse-racing—though she doesn't bet. There are so many activities and so many things to attend to, the Queen Mother could never even consider retiring from public life. And, probably, her loyal public would never let her.

Above all, there is her daughter, the Queen, who has grown into a mature woman and a caring and popular monarch. The Queen Mother must surely be proud of her. Indeed, most people would readily agree that the Queen and the Queen Mother both have a good reason to be proud, each of the other.

Above right: *Making a tour of gardens in South London in 1968, the Queen Mother admires the plants and flowers of Mr. and Mrs. Jamieson in Herne Hill*

Right: *A 75th birthday picture of the Queen Mother and her two eldest grandsons, taken at Royal Lodge, Windsor*

Opposite–Top: *At Princess Anne's christening at Buckingham Palace*

Bottom Left: *Prince Philip, as President of the Royal Society of Arts, bows as he presents the Albert Medal for 1974*

Bottom right: *Extra-mural students at London University give a warm welcome to their Chancellor, the Queen Mother*

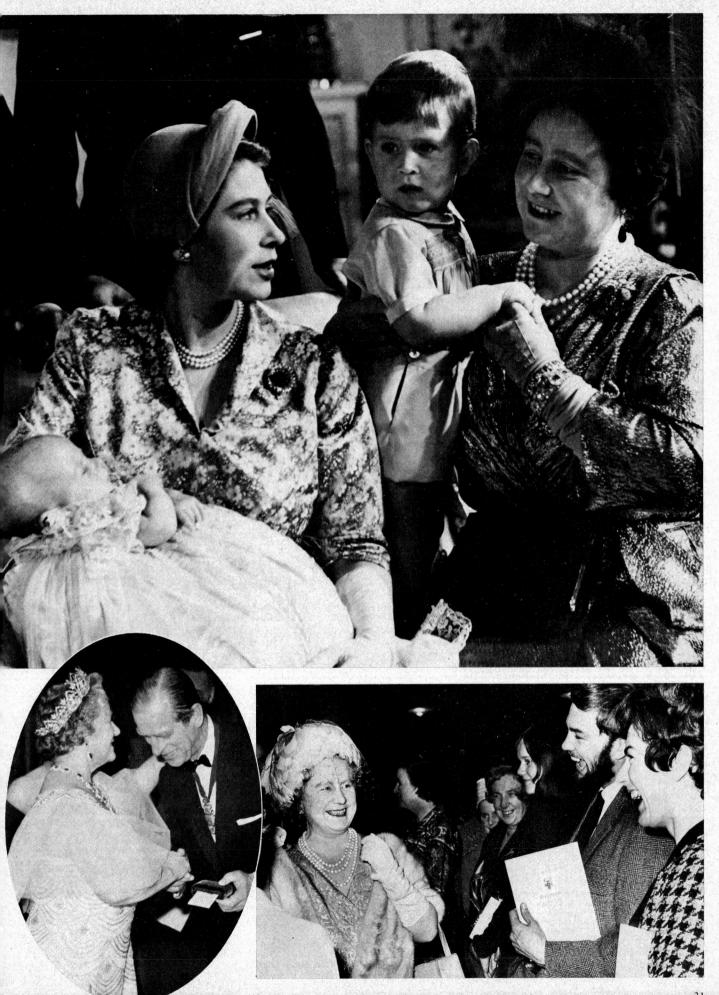

Buckingham Palace

In 1609, as part of a plan to "wean his people from idleness and the enormities thereof", King James I planted four acres of mulberries where Buckingham Palace now stands. He had a scheme to cultivate silk-worms. Unfortunately he made the mistake of choosing the wrong kind of mulberry and the experience was a total disaster. But at least the land remained with the Crown.

The building that stands there today is probably the best-known in the western world—though it has not always been popular with its occupants. Edward VII called Buckingham Palace a "sepulchre" and King George VI described it as "an ice-box".

Prince Philip once referred to the massive 600-roomed building as a "tied cottage" which in a way is what it is, for Buckingham Palace belongs to the nation, not to the Queen personally. And were she ever to abdicate she would presumably move out and make way for her successor.

Originally the Palace was a house, the property of the Duke of Buckingham and Normanby—he was a minor poet who wrote love songs to Princess (later, Queen) Anne around the turn of the 18th century.

Buckingham House was built out of brick, not stone, with wings connected to the central block by curved colonnades. A "little wilderness full of blackbirds and nightingales" spread out on the south side, and the garden at the back was enclosed by a terrace of roses and jasmine, beyond which cattle browsed in long-grassed meadows.

In 1761, the lease of the land had nearly expired and King George III and Queen Charlotte thought the house would make a pleasant family home where they could go when they were not engaged in state functions at St. James's Palace. So the lease was not renewed, and the house was purchased by the Crown for £21,000.

Queen Charlotte, who was only 17 when she married, moved into the house with the King in 1762. While he indulged his passion for clocks and built up the King's Library, (now in the British Museum) the Queen filled the rooms with specially-commissioned work by the finest cabinet-makers and needlewomen.

It was George IV who turned the house into a palace. Or rather the architect John Nash did. He was busy planning Regent Street when, in 1825, he was called to the greater task. Earlier the King had informed him that, "if the public wish to have a palace I have no objection to build one, but I must have a pied-à-terre . . . and I will have it at Buckingham House. There are early associations which endear me to the spot".

So Nash retained the shell of Buckingham's brick house, but built the walls with Bath stone. When the roof was finished the King told his architect: "Nash, the state rooms you have made me are so handsome that I think I shall hold my Courts there." The architect insisted that everything was on too small a scale; he had been building a residence not a state palace. "You know nothing about the matter," said the King, "it will make an excellent palace," and

promptly arranged for his works of art to be brought from his residence at Carlton House.

But the King died before the Palace was ready for occupation, as did William IV who followed him. So it turned out to be the 18-year-old Queen Victoria, on July 13, 1837—three weeks after her accession—who was the first sovereign to take up residence. And Nash was proved right; the place was too small. Edward Blore, who had replaced Nash after a scandal about Nash's cost estimates, added the East Front, later refaced with Portland Stone, which is now the part photographed by tourists as Buckingham Palace—even though it's less than one quarter of the whole.

Buckingham Palace is really a square, with a large courtyard in the centre. Nash's original "front", on the west side, embodies the magnificent State Apartments which look out over nearly 40 acres of garden and lake—the province of Fred Nutbeam who has been a royal gardener for 23 years.

The Royal Family's private apartments are on the first floor, overlooking Green Park—a quarter of a mile away from the kitchens. To make things more practical, early on in the Queen's reign Prince Philip had a small kitchen installed for family meals. But traditions die hard, and main meals are still wheeled along the corridors from the kitchens on heated trolleys.

Apart from the private and State Apartments, Buckingham Palace is like the headquarters of a large firm. It has its own canteen, post office and typists' pool, and with its miles of corridors and hundreds of rooms it is possible for someone to work there for years without ever setting eyes on the Queen.

Above: *The White Drawing Room. There is a concealed door with swinging mirror and table giving access from the Royal Closet and private apartments*
Right: *The Grand Staircase leading to the State Apartments*

Far right: *The thrones, at the end of the Ballroom*
Below right: *The Green Drawing Room, the central room on the east side of the Quadrangle. Three mirror doors lead to the Picture Gallery and, beyond, the Throne Room*

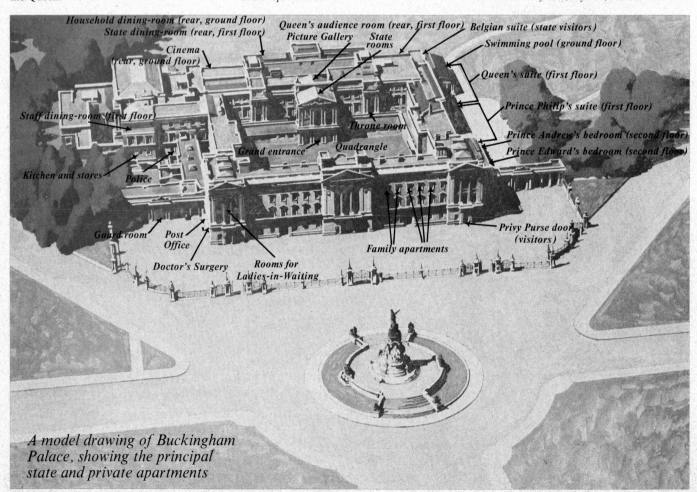

Household dining-room (rear, ground floor)
State dining-room (rear, first floor)
Cinema (rear, ground floor)
Queen's audience room (rear, first floor)
Picture Gallery
State rooms
Belgian suite (state visitors)
Swimming pool (ground floor)
Queen's suite (first floor)
Prince Philip's suite (first floor)
Staff dining-room (first floor)
Throne room
Prince Andrew's bedroom (second floor)
Prince Edward's bedroom (second floor)
Grand entrance
Quadrangle
Kitchen and stores
Police
Guard room
Post Office
Doctor's Surgery
Rooms for Ladies-in-Waiting
Family apartments
Privy Purse door (visitors)

A model drawing of Buckingham Palace, showing the principal state and private apartments

Above left: *The State Dining Room, with seating for 60 guests, was finally completed for Queen Victoria, whose cypher appears in the medallions round the ceiling*

Above: *The Queen's Audience Chamber in the private apartments on the north side*

Below: *The gardens behind Buckingham Palace where the famous Royal Garden Parties take place. This Jubilee year at least three garden parties will be given by the Queen*

Above: *the south side of the Palace, showing the magnificent Nash design and the famous flamingoes that nest on the lake*

Below: *The throne used by Queen Victoria. The legs are very short. But then so was Queen Victoria—she was in fact less than five feet tall*

Right: *The Queen takes the salute at a march-past in 1966 of Her Yeomen of the Guard*

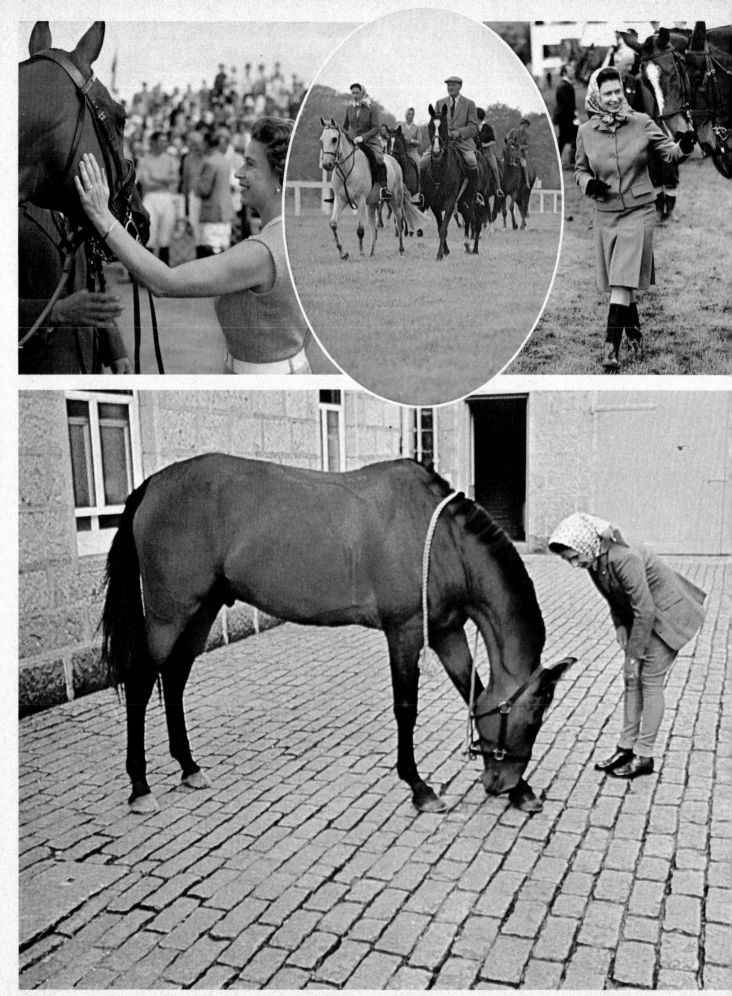

All the Queen's horses...

The night before the Coronation, a lady-in-waiting remarked to the Queen: "Ma'am, you must be feeling apprehensive." Her Majesty nodded, "Yes I am, but I still feel sure my horse will win."

The story is almost certainly apocryphal but it describes so well the Queen's tremendous interest in horses and horse-racing, plus her ability to remain calm in moments when others would almost certainly be a bundle of nerves. (In fact, the Saturday following the Coronation the Queen's horse Aureole came second in the Derby.)

The Queen's interest in flat-racing goes back to childhood when she watched her father's horses winning some of the major events. When King George VI died his daughter inherited the two Royal studs in Norfolk—at Sandringham and Wolverton. She stables her weaned foals and yearlings at Hampton Court and at Polhampton, near Kingsclere in Hampshire. Normally there are about 22 horses in training, divided between Major Dick Hern of West Isley Stables, near Newbury, and Ian Balding of Kingsclere.

The Queen's Racing Manager, with overall responsibility for all her bloodstock interests, is Lord Porchester, heir to the Earl of Carnarvon. For the last four seasons Joe Mercer has had the honour of being the Queen's jockey, winning several races in the royal colours of purple with gold braid and scarlet sleeves. But this year Willie Carson takes over as first jockey to Major Hern—and among Lord Porchester's tips for a place in winners' enclosures this season are Fife And Drum (who won his only two races last year), Rockery and Card Player, who came first in three out of four races in 1976.

Information such as this is well known to the Queen, who is recognised in the racing world as an expert on pedigrees. She keeps a close eye on all that takes place on her studs, and expects her trainers to telephone her with the names of the runners for the following week, usually on a Sunday, and then phone her with the results on the evening of the race.

Over the years the Queen has amassed a considerable fortune in prize money—offsetting the increasingly high cost of owning a string of race horses. In 1957 she was the top-winning owner, collecting altogether £62,211. In 1965 her 17 winners brought in £42,783. But the best year so far was 1974 when one horse alone, Highclere, won £154,000—first in the 1,000 Guineas at Newmarket and the French Oaks at Chantilly, and second to Dahlia in the King George and Queen Elizabeth stakes at Ascot.

The Queen flew over to France specially to see Highclere race at Chantilly and Lord Porchester threw his grey topper high in the air when the horse came in first. The Queen was pleased too . . .

Left: *The Queen has an expert knowledge of horses and their pedigrees, as well as a horse-woman's love of the animals. The picture in the oval was taken in 1962 and shows the Queen leading the traditional morning canter down the course at the start of Ascot week when she invites relatives and close friends to the races and to stay at Windsor Castle*
Right: *At Chester races in May 1966— Garter Lady, a royal entry that did not win*
Below: *Straight from the jockey's mouth— the Queen hears the good news from jockey Joe Mercer after his win on Highclere in the 1,000 Guineas at Newmarket in 1974*
Below right: *The Queen leads her filly Carrozza, with Lester Piggott in the saddle, to the winners' enclosure after the 1957 Epsom Oaks*

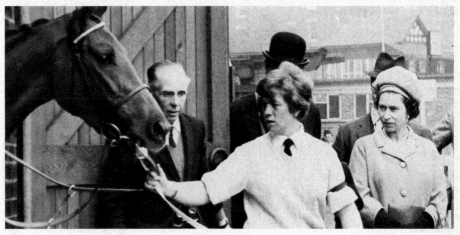

...and all the Queen's men

The Queen is surrounded by men. Out of a total staff of 477 at Buckingham Palace over 300 are men. They serve the Queen and service the monarchy. They are responsible for organising the ceremonial, attending to documents, running the domestic life of the Palace, and making sure the whole complicated machinery of monarchy runs as smoothly and efficiently as the Queen and Prince Philip would wish.

The most impressive title of all is held by Lord Maclean, former Chief Scout, who is the Queen's Lord Chamberlain. His office, with a staff of 23, has charge of the royal library and art collections, and the issuing of royal warrants.

But the man who works closest with the Queen is her Personal Private Secretary, Lieut. Colonel Sir Martin Charteris, who is 63 and has been with Her Majesty ever since she came to the Throne. He travels with the Queen wherever she goes, always on hand to take instructions, to make drafts for her speeches, and to supply information.

An Eton and Sandhurst man, he served with the Rifle Brigade before joining the Palace household, and in his spare time is a talented sculptor. The Deputy Private Secretary, Philip Moore, is a third generation civil servant who is reckoned to be one of the most modern-thinking members of the household—and not just because he was a great admirer of the Rolling Stones a year or two ago.

Vice-Admiral Sir Peter Ashmore is Master of the Household, which means he's in charge of the day-to-day running of the domestic side of the Palace.

It is his job to engage cooks, housekeepers, footmen, and so on and to see that the people he takes on—there are more than 150 altogether—are capable of preparing and serving anything from a small family luncheon to a full-scale banquet.

The Head Chef at the Palace is Peter Page, who has four daughters and lives in Windsor. He has been on the staff for 37 years. Each morning he presents the Queen with a suggested menu for the day—aware that her preference is for good but plain English cooking—and if she wants a change the Queen will put a note at the top.

The financial side of running the Palace is taken care of by a whole department, headed by the Treasurer and Keeper of the Privy Purse, Major Sir Rennie Maudsley. And the task of dealing with the curiosity of the world's press is somehow dealt with by a staff of only six, headed by the Queen's Press Secretary, Ronald Allison, who used to be known as a television sports commentator.

1. *Sir Martin Charteris, the Queen's Private Secretary*
2. *Philip Moore, Deputy Private Secretary*
3. *Ronald Allison, the Press Secretary*
4. *Lord Maclean, the Lord Chamberlain*
5. *Lord Porchester, the Queen's Racing Manager*
6. *Ian Balding, one of the two race horse trainers*
7. *Norman Hartnell, the Queen's fashion designer who was given a knighthood in the 1977 New Year's Honours List*

Opposite—**Top:** *The Queen with Her Yeomen of the Guard, the oldest military regiment in the world*
Bottom: *With Her Grenadier Guards*

Royal destiny

A somewhat demure-looking
Prince Philip at the age of three
and (above) with his parents,
Prince and Princess Andrew of
Greece, on an outing
to the beach

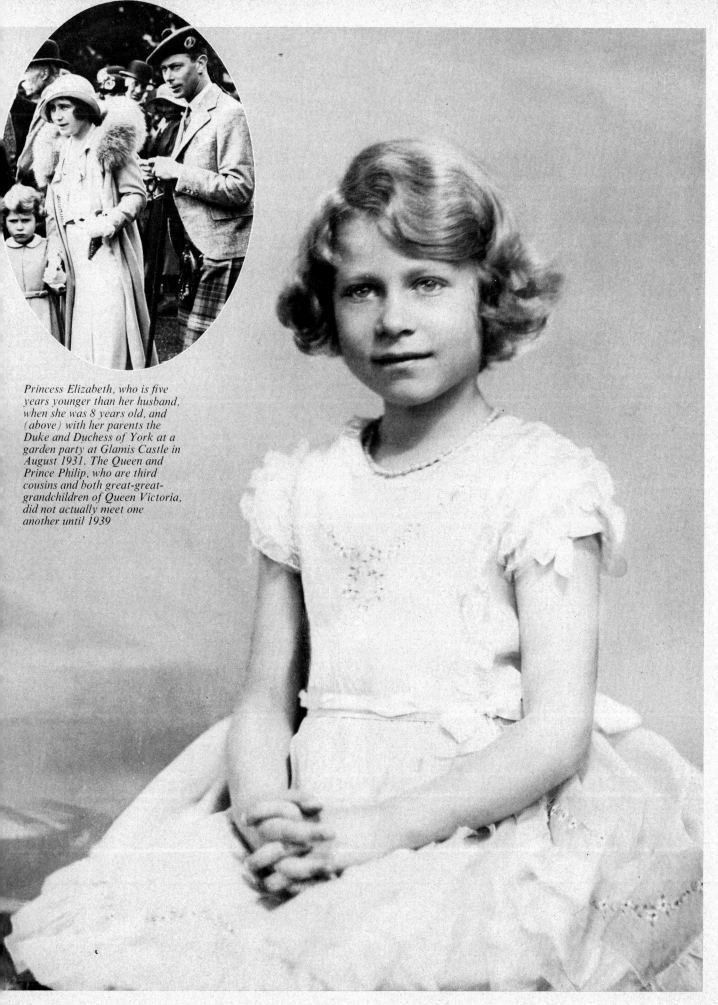

Princess Elizabeth, who is five years younger than her husband, when she was 8 years old, and (above) with her parents the Duke and Duchess of York at a garden party at Glamis Castle in August 1931. The Queen and Prince Philip, who are third cousins and both great-great-grandchildren of Queen Victoria, did not actually meet one another until 1939

Love and marriage

Neither the Queen nor Prince Philip has ever mentioned in public how they came to meet and fall in love. But the story is that Prince and Princess pledged themselves to one another on an August afternoon in 1946 while strolling by the banks of Loch Muick, near Balmoral, and that Princess Elizabeth was secretly in love with the handsome sailor Prince long before that—when she was only 16 or 17 and he was a wartime visitor to Windsor Castle.

Contrary to what most people believe, Prince Philip is not Greek by blood but was born a member of both the Danish and Greek royal families. His grandfather was Prince William of Denmark—elected King of Greece—whose sister, Alexandra, married the Prince of Wales, who later became King Edward VII.

Philip was born in a villa on Corfu in June 1921, the only son of Prince Andrew of Greece and Princess Alice of Battenberg. His parents, who did not always get on, eventually separated. And because his mother was often ill, Philip spent much of his childhood in England with his grandmother, the Dowager Marchioness of Milford Haven. He went to Cheam School then Gordonstoun, and later entered Dartmouth Naval College in 1939 as a cadet. In 1941, as a junior officer aboard a battleship, he saw action against the Italian fleet off Cape Matapan and was awarded a mention in despatches.

The first time Prince Philip and his future wife were photographed together was at Dartmouth in 1939 when he was an 18-year-old cadet and Princess Elizabeth was 13. But they didn't really get to know one another till three or four years later when, as a fully-blown first lieutenant, he was invited to spend some of his leave at Windsor and at Coppins, the home of the late Duke and Duchess of Kent. On Elizabeth's 18th birthday Philip was a guest at the family luncheon party at Windsor Castle and, shortly after, his photograph appeared on Princess Elizabeth's mantlepiece. Her governess thought the picture might prompt gossip, so it was taken down and replaced a few weeks later by one of a bearded naval officer—which the Princess laughingly suggested made him incognito!

From the start it was almost a fairy-tale romance of a Princess and a wartime sailor. But it was not without its problems. For one thing, although England had been practically his home since he was eight, Prince Philip was still a Greek national. He wanted to become a naturalised British subject, not least because he wished to continue his career in the Royal Navy after the war. But political complications to do with the future of the monarchy in Greece led to his application being deferred time and again.

Also, although King George VI and Queen Elizabeth liked Philip, they thought it too soon for their elder daughter to make a choice.

In 1944, the two kings—George II of Greece and George VI—discussed the possibility of the marriage. But Princess Elizabeth's parents discouraged the idea. "We both think she is too young for that now," the King wrote to his mother, Queen Mary. "She has never met any young men of her own age."

Three years later, it was obvious that the two young people were very much in love. There were rumours of an engagement, but still there were objectors to Philip's nationality. And others, so soon after the war, were sensitive to the fact that his four sisters had all married Germans.

A three-month royal tour to South Africa had been planned to start in February 1947 and the King decided that both his daughters should accompany him and the Queen.

It was a long and painful separation for the Prince and the Princess. But at least while the Royal Family were away, Prince Philip received an excellent piece of news—his naturalisation papers had come through, and he was now a British subject. Princess Elizabeth celebrated her 21st birthday in Cape Town, and sailed for home three days later, overjoyed at the prospect of seeing Philip again.

Her parents now gave their whole-hearted blessing to the union, and while a little more time had to pass before an engagement could officially be announced, the young naval lieutenant's sports car was often parked in the Palace courtyard.

The official announcement of the engagement came on July 9, 1947: "It is with the greatest pleasure that the King and Queen announce the betrothal of their dearly beloved daughter . . ." That evening huge crowds gathered in front of Buckingham Palace singing, "All the nice girls love a sailor".

Above: *The camera catches Prince Philip and Princess Elizabeth at a wedding in 1946, at which the Princess was a bridesmaid*
Below: *Probably the first picture of the Queen and Prince Philip together, taken at Dartmouth Naval College in July 1939. Prince Philip is standing at the back, next to his uncle Lord Mountbatten*
Bottom left: *Princess Elizabeth, after she became engaged, arriving at a ball in Edinburgh*
Bottom right: *At the Palace on the day of their engagement*

1

2

3

4

5

By Royal Appointment

The royal coat of arms above a shop or factory, with the coveted words "By Appointment" underneath doesn't necessarily mean that the Queen herself uses the product. For instance, Dunhill and Benson & Hedges may supply cigarettes to Buckingham Palace for the benefit of guests but it is known that the Queen is a non-smoker.

However, by scanning the list of over 1,000 royal warrant-holders it's possible to get an idea of the Royal Family's likes, eating habits, taste in clothes and preference in many other directions.

For example, it would appear from the list that the Queen sleeps in a Sleepeezee or Slumberland bed, wakes up to a cup of Twinings tea, enjoys Kellogg's Corn Flakes, bathes with Yardley or Pears soap before putting on a Horrockses dress and a Pringle cardigan. She wears a Burberry coat and, tying her Liberty silk scarf over her head, she feeds her corgis with Spratt's dog food before taking them for a walk wearing her James Allan and Son (Edinburgh) shoes.

While she's out her letters are typed on Imperial typewriters, her piano is taken care of by Broadwoods, and her pork pies are delivered from Henry Telfer of Northampton. Some appointments reflect the Queen's love of country life: weavers, gum boot makers, horse-box manufacturers—all feature in the royal warrant-holders list.

If a trader is lucky enough to do business near a royal residence he stands a better chance of being granted a royal warrant. In Ballater, near Balmoral Castle, the village baker, butcher, chemist and seller of fishing tackle are all listed, as are the kilt-makers, the local garage and the laundry at nearby Aberdeen.

The system of royal warrants dates back over 800 years, the first to be documented being granted to the Weaver Company by Henry II in 1155. Nearly four centuries later, Henry VIII drew up a special statute "for the good order of his household", naming his

favourite suppliers and allowing them certain rights.

But some things—such as neon signs proclaiming royal patronage—are not allowed. And, though it's unusual, holders of royal warrants can be struck off the list. In 1975, as a result of "rationalisation", some 70 firms were asked to take down their signs by January 1, 1979.

From January this year, tradesmen who make "a continuous, satisfactory and direct supply of goods or services" to Prince Charles will be able to apply for the Royal Warrant of Appointment.

Incidentally, being a royal warrant-holder doesn't mean that the manufacturers supply goods to the Palace free. The Queen is expected to pay her bills like anyone else.

6

7   8

9

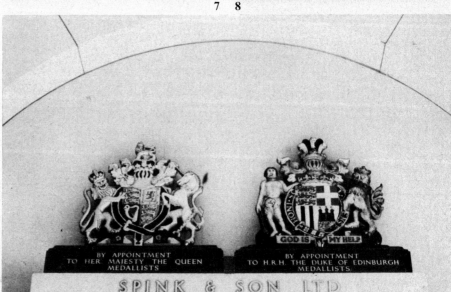

1. *Baxters of Morecambe, Lancs.—Purveyors of potted shrimps to the Queen and the Queen Mother*
2. *Garrards, Regent Street, London—Goldsmiths and Crown Jewellers to the Queen*
3. *Rigby and Peller, South Molton Street, London—Corsetiers to the Queen*
4. *Harrods of Knightsbridge—Provisioners of household goods to the Queen; Outfitters to the Duke of Edinburgh; Suppliers of china, glass and fancy goods to the Queen Mother*
5. *Whitbreads of London—Suppliers of beer to the Queen*
6. *Hamleys, Regent Street—Toy and sports merchants to the late Queen Mary*
7. *Woods Pharmacy, High Street, Windsor—Pharmaceutical Chemist to the Queen*
8. *John F. Renshaw of Mitcham, Surrey—Purveyors of almond products to the Queen Mother*
9. *Spinks of King Street, St. James's, London—Suppliers of medals to the Queen*

Princess Elizabeth's wedding

Above: *Waving from Buckingham Palace balcony after returning from Westminster Abbey. On the Princess's right is the best man, the Marquess of Milford Haven*
Below: *The wedding cake, weighing 500 lb.*
Bottom: *The Archbishop of Canterbury, the late Dr. Fisher, performing the wedding ceremony*

When Princess Elizabeth and the Duke of Edinburgh were married on November 20, 1947, life in Britain was still plagued by wartime rationing. Coupons were needed to buy clothes and petrol, furniture bore a Government mark to show it was "utility", and fuel was in such short supply that families huddled around their pathetically small coal fires wearing ex-service-men's duffel coats.

Most people welcomed the sparkling celebrations and spectacle of a royal wedding as a relief from boring austerity. On the eve of the wedding London's biggest crowds since the coronation of King George VI gathered outside Buckingham Palace chanting "We want the Bride" and the following day it was estimated that over 100,000 well-wishers around the Victoria Memorial waited for the royal procession to set out for Westminster Abbey. The country might still be grappling with post-war shortages, and be critical of needless extravagance, but as Winston Churchill said: "Millions will welcome this joyous event as a flash of colour on the hard road we have to travel."

There was another reason why people welcomed the wedding, sleeping out on the freezing pavements along the route to get a good view, searching in every shop for a Union Jack to wave. Princess Elizabeth, young and attractive, represented people's hopes for the future. Her parents had been a symbol for millions of fighting service-men and bomb-blitzed families during the war. They wanted to give the King and Queen's elder daughter a good send-off. And they liked the look of the young man she had chosen. He might not be a native-born Englishman, but he had spent most of his life in Britain and had seen action in the Royal Navy. There was something about him, a sort of breezy manliness, that bode well for the future.

The wedding was to take place in Westminster Abbey. There were to be eight bridesmaids, including Princess Margaret and Princess Alexandra, and two pages, the little Princes William of Gloucester and Michael of Kent. Norman Hartnell was given the honour of designing the dress—and went about the task in such secrecy that he not only curtained off his work-room but also white-washed the windows. Wedding presents arrived from all over the world—a full-length mink coat from Canada, a filly

from the Aga Khan, a golden coffee service from the Emir of Transjordan.

The King and Queen gave their daughter two pearl necklaces joined together by a pearl clasp, and a ruby and diamond necklace. Queen Mary gave her grand-daughter a diamond tiara, bracelets and a brooch. And Princess Margaret, who as yet had few family heirlooms to pass on, gave her sister a fully-equipped picnic basket. (Sadly, Queen Mary was not to live long enough to see her grand-daughter Elizabeth crowned Queen, but she did have the great joy of seeing her first great-grandchildren, Charles and Anne.)

The morning of the wedding itself dawned grey, cold and misty. But inside Buckingham Palace there were enough last-minute crises to make anyone warm. Just two hours before the bride was due to leave for the Abbey, the frame of the diamond tiara she planned to wear over her veil snapped as she was putting it on. It was rushed away to the royal jewellers for repair and returned just in time. Then it was discovered that the two pearl necklaces, which the Princess specially wanted to wear, had been put on display with the other wedding presents at St. James's Palace. A secretary was despatched to fetch them. Finally the bride's bouquet, of all things, went missing—it eventually turned up in a cupboard.

However, precisely on time at 11.15 the crowds outside the Palace cheered and shouted as the Princess and her father set out for the Abbey in the Irish State Coach, escorted by the Household Cavalry—wearing for the first time since before the war their full dress uniform.

As the King and his daughter entered Westminster Abbey and paused at the door, a fanfare of silver trumpets rang round the great church, and the whole congregation bowed to this slender man in an admiral's uniform, and his daughter, the Princess, pale but composed. Father and daughter proceeded up the aisle to the music of Praise My Soul, The King Of Heaven, one of the bride's favourite hymns. The King later wrote in a letter: "I was so proud and thrilled at having you so close to me on our long walk in Westminster Abbey."

"Who giveth this woman?" asked the Archbishop of Canterbury; the King took his daughter's hand and held it forward.

"Notwithstanding the splendour and national significance of the service in this Abbey," said the Archbishop in his address, "it is in all essentials the same as it would be for any cottager who might be married this afternoon in some small country church in a remote village in the dales. The same vows are taken, the same prayers are offered, and the same blessings are given."

It was true, and yet it was not. Few weddings could have been as richly splendid as this one. But there were moments which were unrehearsed and not included in any plan. As when, just before the wedding march, Princess Elizabeth, now wife but still a daughter, sank billowing in a deep and grateful curtsy to her father, the King.

At Buckingham Palace, 150 guests sat down to the wedding breakfast and beside each plate was a sprig of white heather gathered at Balmoral. Just for luck.

Above: *Lieutenant Philip Mountbatten, RN, with Princess Elizabeth, his bride, leaving Buckingham Palace for their honeymoon*
Below: *The Royal Special Licence issued from the Faculty Office of the Archbishop of Canterbury. Attached to the wedding licence is a six-inch square seal of the Court of Faculties*

Even on honeymoon, Prince Philip and Princess Elizabeth could not always be alone. On the right (top) is Birkhall, near Balmoral, where they spent the second part of their honeymoon and, below, Broadlands, in Hampshire, where they stayed the first night. Broadlands is the home of Lord Louis Mountbatten, Prince Philip's uncle

Royal honeymoon

Only two years after the war, with peacetime austerity biting into everyone's pockets, it would have been thought unpatriotic for Princess Elizabeth and her husband to spend their honeymoon abroad, or in some other expensive way. So, for the first part at least, they went to stay at the bridegroom's uncle's house at Romsey in Hampshire.

Broadlands had been associated with the Mountbatten family for many years. Lord Louis Mountbatten's wife, Edwina—a grand-daughter of Queen Victoria's Prime Minister Lord Palmerston—had been born there. She and Lord Mountbatten had spent their own honeymoon in the house. So they were very happy to offer their home, or at least a wing of it, to Princess Elizabeth—the other part of the house was still being used as a wartime convalescent home.

Fires were lit, a meal was prepared, and everything was made to look as welcoming as possible for the bride and bridegroom when they arrived in the late afternoon of November 20, 1947. They had left Buckingham Palace following the wedding reception bound for Waterloo station in an open coach,

padded in with hot water bottles and with Princess Elizabeth's corgi snuggling at her feet.

The newly-wedded couple spent a long weekend at Broadlands, attending Sunday worship at Romsey Abbey and strolling in the late autumn sunshine through the grounds (this was partly for the benefit of the press camera-men who could see the house from the road and had maintained an almost 24-hour vigil).

The Prince and Princess had been overwhelmed by the amount of interest in their wedding, and by the generosity of people who had sent them almost every kind of present from a refrigerator (a gift of the Women's Voluntary Service) to a cloth of lace which had been crocheted by Mahatma Gandhi himself.

They were specially grateful to the Princess's parents who, from the start, had welcomed Philip into their home, and during their honeymoon they sat down to write a letter of thanks. King George VI's reply is couched in words that very much reflect his deep love for his daughter. "I am so glad you wrote and told Mummy that you think the

long wait before your engagement . . . was for the best. I was rather afraid you had thought I was being hard-hearted about it". . . .
"Your leaving us has left a great blank in our lives but do remember that your old home is still yours and do come back to it as much and as often as possible. I can see you are sublimely happy with Philip which is right, but don't forget us is the wish of
Your ever loving and devoted Papa."

Before leaving Broadlands the newly-weds wrote a message thanking "countrymen and well-wishers in all parts of the world" for their loving interest on the wedding day. "We can find no words to express what we feel, but we can at least offer our grateful thanks to the millions who have given us this unforgettable send-off in our married life."

From Broadlands they travelled to Birkhall, now the Queen Mother's house on Deeside, where Princess Elizabeth had spent many happy childhood summers. Unfortunately, in November it was sleeting and snowing hard. The Duke of Edinburgh developed a bad cold and spent much of the time in bed being nursed by his wife.

Cars, planes and trains

Cars are not something the Queen gets madly excited about. On official engagements she likes a stately limousine that will allow the public a good view of their monarch. In private she's happy with her 3.5 litre Rover saloon (JGY 280) which she bought in 1961—the same year as Prince Philip purchased his 3 litre Alvis. (He has since sold it and now drives a sturdy Range Rover.)

Prince Charles drives an Aston Martin DB6, and Princess Anne still has her Reliant Scimitar with the number plate 1420 H—the number and initial of the 14th/20th Hussars, of which she is Colonel-in-Chief. The Regiment bought the number from a United Dairies milk float as a 21st birthday present to the Princess. Captain Mark Phillips owns one of the new Rovers.

There are six limousines for official use in the Royal Mews: a Rolls-Royce Phantom IV which was a wedding present from the RAF, two Phantom Vs, a Jubilee Landolet Rolls-Royce, and two black Austin Princesses. And the appearance of any one of these has people craning forward to see who's inside.

With a husband and two sons who are qualified pilots (though, admittedly, Prince Andrew's qualification so far is for gliders), it would be surprising if the Queen did not make a great deal of use of aircraft to speed her around the country on official visits. She quite enjoys flying, but she has never ventured up in a helicopter—though there is no safety rule that restricts the monarch from doing so. The only rule is that the Queen and Prince Charles never fly in the same aircraft, in case of accident.

There are two helicopters in the Queen's Flight, used by Prince Philip especially, and three shiny red Andovers, based at the RAF station at Benson, Oxfordshire. About 100 service-men and civilians are needed to operate the Flight, which altogether costs about £1 million a year to run. But besides the Queen, other members of the Royal Family, Service Chiefs of Staff, certain Government Ministers and visiting heads of state are eligible to make use of the aircraft.

Edward VIII founded the Flight in 1936 and it was Queen Victoria who made the first royal train journey. The Royal Family pay for all their personal train travel—but the carriages, very often attached to a normal service train, are provided by British Rail and cost several thousand pounds a year to maintain.

For the past two years work has been going on at British Rail's Wolverton coach-works in Buckinghamshire refurbishing the royal coaches and constructing two new "day saloons" for the Queen and Prince Philip at an officially estimated cost of £500,000. It is expected that the spanking new train, with its kitchen, dining-room, bedrooms and sophisticated telephone system, will be used extensively during the Queen's round-Britain visits in Jubilee Year.

Above: *The Queen at the wheel, driving in text-book style, with a young Princess Anne at her side*
Below: *Not on the official list of royal transport—Prince Charles is given a ride in the Scilly Isles in 1967*

Top: *The "bubble" roof of a royal limousine that gives everyone the chance of a clear view of the Queen*
Above: *The unmistakable red of one of the helicopters of the Queen's Flight*
Above right: *Prince Philip at the controls of an aircraft of the Queen's Flight in 1971, with his personal standard at the mast-head on the roof*
Right: *Setting out for New Year at Sandringham in the royal train from Liverpool Street, London. With Prince Andrew and Prince Edward is Lady Sarah Armstrong-Jones*
Left: *A 1900 Daimler Tonneau belonging to Edward VII*
Far left: *Princess Anne's Scimitar, with its distinctive registration*

The Queen's first child

In the words of the Home Secretary's official announcement: "Her Royal Highness, the Princess Elizabeth, Duchess of Edinburgh, was safely delivered of a Prince at 9.14 this evening, November 14, 1948. Her Royal Highness and the infant Prince are both well."

Prince Charles was born on a Sunday of mist and rain. The birth took place in the Buhl Room at Buckingham Palace, used only two days earlier for a thorough examination of the already ailing King George VI. Prince Philip spent much of the waiting time playing frantic squash in the basement with his friend and Private Secretary Michael Parker.

The King's illness meant that his daughter had to fulfil many of his engagements, but she made time each day to play with her children—Princess Anne was born almost two years later. They were brought to her each day from 9 to 9.30 a.m., and after tea Princess Elizabeth and her husband went to the nursery for an hour or so before the Princess bathed her children and tucked them up in bed.

Princess Elizabeth wanted her son's childhood to be as happy and carefree as her own had been, but after the King's death and her accession to the Throne, this became more difficult to guarantee. As heir to the Throne the Prince was bound to be in the public eye. As a small boy however, he seems to have been fairly unconcerned by any fuss. He showed none of the imperiousness of his sister, although—like his grandfather—he had a quick but short-lived temper.

The first major decision that the Queen and Prince Philip had to make regarding their son was about his education. In common with royal practice, the Queen had

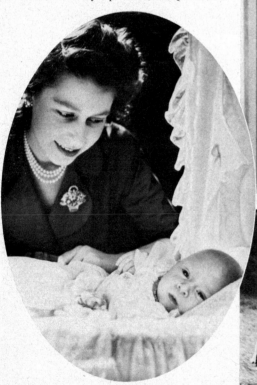

Above: *The Queen with her first child, aged one month, in the first official picture*
Above right: *This picture was specially taken at Balmoral to celebrate Prince Charles' fourth birthday, in 1952*
Right: *Running free, on the farm at Balmoral when Prince Charles was eight*

been educated by governesses. But Prince Philip had gone to boarding schools, and the question arose: in a modern democracy shouldn't the heir to the Throne have the opportunity of mixing with a wide group of young people, as soon as possible?

In the end it was decided to break with tradition, to the extent that Charles would say goodbye to his governess and begin school, though not until he was eight. He went to Hill House, a small private school in Knightsbridge, and then to his father's old school, Cheam, on the Berkshire downs. His first school report showed he was "very good indeed" at reading, "loved" history, and in singing lessons displayed "a sweet voice, especially in lower register."

At Cheam, where he was not always very happy, Charles managed to get chicken pox—which he passed on to his sister—and not long after he was rushed to hospital to have his appendix removed.

When the time came to move on from Cheam—a preparatory school where most pupils finished between 13 and 14—the question of his future arose once more. His name had been put down for Eton, at birth, and most of his school friends were going on to Charterhouse. But Charles was not all

Above left: *This charming study of Prince Charles and Princess Anne with their grandparents, King George and Queen Elizabeth, was taken on Prince Charles' third birthday*

Far left: *Taking his first photograph—of the Queen and Princess Anne—at Balmoral*

Left: *Facing a battery of cameras as well as a new term at the Knightsbridge school he attended as a day-boy in 1957*

Above: *Even on holiday at Balmoral, in 1964, Prince Charles runs into a cameraman as he leaves a fishing tackle shop in Ballater*
Left: *When he was on a tour of the Scilly Isles in 1967 school-children had a chance of talking with their future King*

THE QUEEN'S FIRST CHILD *continued*

that keen on going to either of these famous schools, and his father—always the most forward-thinking of the family—pressed for his own old school, Gordonstoun. And so it was decided.

Prince Charles was never quite as at home at Gordonstoun as his father had been. At that time he was a much more introspective person, able to express himself on the stage, but not quite as ebullient as his father on the sports field. Academically he was not brilliant; fascinated by history but flattened by mathematics. When, at 17, he had the chance to do an exchange with a boy from Geelong School in Victoria, Australia, Prince Charles welcomed the opportunity of a change.

And the change undoubtedly did him good. He emerged after six months much more of a person in his own right, and he found a warm attachment for Australia that will probably never leave him. He returned to Gordonstoun to finish off his schooling, and was promptly made guardian of the school and earned a silver medal in the Duke of Edinburgh's Award Scheme.

The next stage in his education—remembering that Prince Charles' main job in life was decided for him in the moment he was born—was to go up to Trinity College, Cambridge, where he studied archaeology and anthropology. After three years he gained a second class Bachelor of Arts degree in history.

By now he was 21, an age when some men, but by no means all, have developed their personalities almost to the full. Charles still had about him an immature and at times almost sullen look. Shyer than either his father or his sister—even though he enjoyed playing the fool in university revues—he had, like his grandfather and his mother, a quick sensitivity to other people's feelings. But he sometimes lacked the confidence to express the views that, deep down, he felt most strongly. The assured, wise-cracking Prince Charles whom every girl noticed, instead of merely noting, had still to emerge.

Above left: *Prince Charles spent six months in the Australian outback, as an exchange student, in 1966*
Above: *For once unnoticed Prince Charles goes shopping in Cambridge*
Right: *The Prince takes to cycling in his undergraduate days*
Below: *Prince Charles' study at Buckingham Palace in 1969—it has since been completely restyled to his own design*
Far right: *This picture was taken at Windsor in 1969—the year the Queen's eldest son was invested as Prince of Wales*

56

"Our daughter, Princess Anne"

No child is the image of one parent, but if Prince Charles' personality is akin to his mother's, then Princess Anne in many ways takes after her father.

Both of them have a forthright manner, a strong desire to see things done their way, and a sense of humour that is sharp and not always entirely kind. On the more creditable side perhaps, they share a reputation for being extremely courageous—few women would take the knocks that Princess Anne has taken and still continue horse-riding—and of being very enthusiastic and conscientious when they're engaged on something that really interests them. There is nothing wishy-washy about either Prince Philip or his daughter.

Princess Anne, fourth in line to the Throne after Charles, Andrew and Edward, was born on August 15, 1950, at Clarence House—the only one of the Queen and Prince Philip's children to be born there. Her mother came to the Throne when Anne was 18 months old and, until her marriage in

Above left: *More than 100 pictures were taken at Princess Anne's first official "sitting". This one, with Prince Charles, was taken in September 1950*
Left: *Princess Anne—a bridesmaid several times—at the wedding of Lady Pamela Mountbatten to Mr. David Hicks in 1960*
Below: *At Frogmore, Windsor, with a favourite pet*

Above: *The Queen and Princess Anne with the Welsh pony Greensleeves at Windsor in December 1959*
Below: *Proudly showing off her uniform when she first joined the Brownies*
Right: *Again on Greensleeves—the Princess who was to grow up to become such a world-renowned horse-woman and even a competitor in the Olympic Games*

Left: *Princess Anne taking Goodwill through the water at the final selection trial for the Olympics at Osberton, Nottinghamshire, in June 1976*
Above: *Going to church at Benenden, Kent in 1963, shortly after joining Benenden school*
Below: *A bridesmaid for the sixth time, at the wedding of Lady Elizabeth Anson at Westminster Abbey in 1972*
Right: *Princess Anne, at 21*

1973, the Princess spent most of her life at Buckingham Palace.

Like all three of her brothers, Anne took her first nursery school lessons from "Mispy", the name the Royal children gave to the small, dark-haired Catherine Peebles, who came from Glasgow. She had previously been governess to their cousin Prince Michael of Kent.

As a child Charles was sensitive to criticism or harsh words, retreating into a shell, but from the start his sister appears to have been worried by very few people. Whereas Prince Charles never copied his mother's childhood caper of passing and re-passing the Palace guardsmen for the fun of seeing them salute, Princess Anne discovered the game almost as soon as she could walk. She was never a girl for playing with dolls, much preferring her corgi Sherry, and two South American love-birds called David and Annie, one of which she painstakingly trained to perch on a stick held at arm's length.

Her love of horses—and here she did follow her mother—showed itself very early on when she learned to ride at Windsor and at Balmoral. But it was never enough just to ride; Anne wanted to compete, to accomplish enough skill to do well in her own right at gymkhanas and then at horse trials and in three-day eventing.

Prince Charles has never shown such enthusiasm in this area—though he enjoys polo—and although they have always had a strong brother-sister love for one another, they have recognised since they were children that their characters are quite dissimilar.

Anne envied her brother leaving home for boarding school, and she could hardly wait for the time when in 1963—at the age of 13—she joined the 320 pupils at Benenden School, in Kent. She seems to have enjoyed school life much more than Prince Charles did, though she could soon become bored by some lessons and was happiest out of doors.

For a time after she left school Princess Anne went through a stage—like most ex-students of a single-sex school—of discovering which clothes suited her best, which hair-style was the right one, and which kind of men she liked—and which she didn't. She enjoyed pop music and liked parties, but didn't go to that many. And sometimes, as she began playing a larger part in the round of royal duties, she looked distinctly fed up.

But all this passed. As the swinging (and confusing) Sixties moved into the Seventies, Princess Anne seemed to find herself. She worked hard for the Save The Children Fund as their President, as Patron of the Riding For The Disabled Association, and other charities.

The Queen gave her a chestnut colt, Doublet, as a birthday present and she rode to victory, becoming not only European Champion in 1971, but also BBC Sports Personality of the Year at 21. Later, of course, she was to earn a place in the British Equestrian Olympic Team.

Everyone waited for Princess Anne to fall in love and get married. But as she said: "One of the myths of my career is that people have written over the years that the only thing I wanted to do when I left school was get married. It was one of my bugbears. It couldn't have been further from the truth." She made the point in an interview—after she became engaged to Captain Mark Phillips.

The royal yacht

Since she was launched in 1953 the royal yacht Britannia has steamed hundreds of thousands of miles, taking the Royal Family on official visits and holidays all over the world. It has been the scene of two honeymoons—Princess Margaret's and Princess Anne's—and has been used as a luxurious entertainment centre for export-boosting business-men.

When the Queen sails in Britannia she usually takes about 30 of her staff from Buckingham Palace. To run the ship there is a crew of 21 officers and 256 ratings, the majority of whom belong to the permanent Royal Yacht Service. Their cap ribbons carry the words "Royal Yacht", with a gold crown between the words, and unlike Royal Navy sailors they wear their serge jumpers inside instead of outside their trousers. Another difference is that no punishments are handed out aboard. If a sailor gets into trouble he is simply returned to normal naval service.

Over the years the expense of keeping Britannia in service has brought almost constant criticism from various quarters. It costs approximately £5,500 a week to keep the ship sitting in dock, and almost twice that amount to operate at sea. Since her launching she's undergone nine refits—the most recent in 1974 at an estimated cost of £1·75 million—but though Britannia is extremely expensive there are many who say that on a state visit or official tour of the Commonwealth it is the most fitting and imposing form of transport for a Queen.

Britannia is really a floating palace where the Queen can entertain foreign heads of state, and where she can also rest between engagements on a heavy royal tour. The fact that she remains aboard instead of moving into a British Embassy or private house does reduce costs.

The ship contains an elegant drawing-room—approached down a wide mahogany staircase—which, along with an ante-room, is large enough to accommodate 200 guests. There is also a magnificent dining-room and a cinema.

The Queen and Prince Philip each have a private sitting-room—the Queen's with white walls and moss green carpet, Prince Philip's with grey carpet and teak panelling. A lift connects these rooms to the royal bedrooms on the next deck up. Overlooking the stern is a sun lounge where the Queen likes to have breakfast—when the sea is calm. Even with stabilisers, Britannia has been known to give its royal passengers a rough voyage.

Above: *The dining-room, and the Queen's and Prince Philip's rooms, aboard Britannia*
Below: *The Queen, talking with her Private Secretary, Sir Martin Charteris, has one of the famous red despatch boxes on her knee*
Right: *With Pierre Trudeau, Prime Minister of Canada, and the leaders of Canadian Provinces on board Britannia in 1976*

Early royal tours

The Queen has travelled more miles and seen more countries than any other British monarch and she has almost certainly talked to more prime ministers and presidents than any other head of state.

To give an idea, between 1952 and the end of 1966 the total distance covered by the Queen on royal tours abroad amounted to a staggering 178,753 miles, more than seven times the circumference of the earth.

Altogether she called on 56 countries and islands, and at a conservative estimate shook hands with about 70,000 people. She was greeted by people wearing almost anything from full dress uniform to a loin-cloth, and travelled in every kind of transport from a bullet-proof limousine to a rowing boat.

From each visit the Queen returned home laden with a marvellous assortment of gifts and, besides giving presents in return, left behind warm memories of a smiling lady who possessed great charm and dignity.

By far the most ambitious tour the Queen has ever undertaken was the one she embarked on only a few months after the Coronation. In November 1953 she and Prince Philip left for a tour that was to last 173 days and cover over 40,000 miles.

The tour began in the West Indies, where the royal party joined the liner Gothic, and continued through the Panama Canal to Fiji. On the beautiful Pacific island of Tonga the Queen and Prince Philip renewed their friendship with Queen Salote, whose good humour had made such an impression at the Coronation. Then they travelled on to New Zealand where they spent Christmas—in fact it was from Auckland that the Queen made her Christmas Day broadcast.

In February 1954 the Gothic steamed into Sydney harbour to a tumultuous welcome from the Australian people. During the next two months the Royal party travelled as far north as the Great Barrier Reef, and as far west as Perth. After the Queen had opened her first Australian Parliament—wearing her Coronation gown—Mr. Robert Menzies, the Prime Minister, assured her at a banquet: "Skilled as you are in the noble arts of Queenship, young though you are in years, may I say to you—you can count on us."

The return route from the other side of the world was by way of the Cocos Islands and Ceylon, and then across the Indian ocean to Aden. From there the royal party flew to Entebbe, where the Queen had begun the flight home after her father's death. This time she was to open a dam.

Away from England for almost six months, the Queen and Prince Philip had greatly missed seeing their children—even more so because Princess Anne, who was three, and Prince Charles, five, were both at a particularly interesting age. So the royal couple were thrilled when the little Prince and Princess were waiting to greet them on board Britannia, at Tobruk in North Africa, at the final stages of their trip. The children had sailed from Portsmouth and stayed in Malta with Lord and Lady Mountbatten, to await their parents' arrival.

From Tobruk the united family travelled

home, via Malta and Gibraltar, and came up the Thames to Tower Bridge. Everyone agreed, it had been the most successful royal tour ever undertaken.

But it was by no means the last of the Queen's travels abroad. During the next 11 years she made state visits to several countries including America (1957), Iran and Italy (1961), and Germany (1965).

In 1956 Prince Philip made a round-the-world trip, during which he opened the Olympic Games in Melbourne and visited the Antarctic. And again, in 1959, he flew off on a 100-day tour that took him to India, the Far East and the Pacific.

Almost as soon as he got back he and the Queen set out once more, this time to Canada and 16,000 miles of travelling with more than 40 overnight stops. As if her travels were not tiring enough in itself, the Queen confided to the Canadian Prime Minister early on in the tour that she was expecting her third child. But she refused even to contemplate any curtailment of the heavy schedule. After all, as she had pointed out to someone before she left England: "I'm not going on holiday but to work."

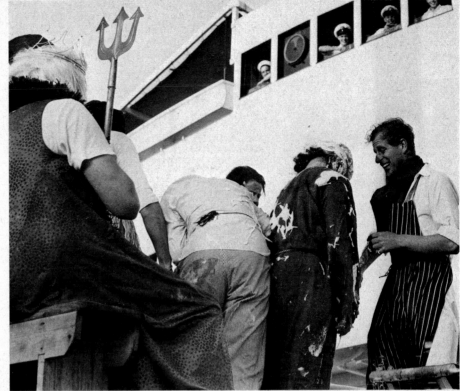

*Opposite—***Top:** *In Western Australia, 1954, bouquets were placed on a stool instead of being handed to the Queen because of a polio scare* **Bottom:** *With the Governor of Bermuda in 1953*

Above: *The "crossing the line" ceremony aboard the Gothic* **Oval:** *Calling on the magnificent Queen Salote* **Left:** *With Australian service-men of two wars* **Below left:** *Taking leave of Malta in 1954* **Below:** *Fascinated by one of the famous apes on the Rock of Gibraltar*

Top left: *A Fijian chief invites the Queen to land at Suva Bay in 1953*
Above: *Sailing up the Thames at the end of the tour*
Oval: *Opening the Canadian Parliamentary Session in 1957—the first reigning monarch ever to do so*
Bottom left: *New York's reception in 1957*
Below: *A linguist's stick, a gift from Ghana*
Left: *Coming home to a warm welcome in 1954*

Above: *Entering a replica of the first successful British village in America at Jamestown, U.S.A.*
Above right: *Boy scouts greet the Queen in Sierra Leone in 1961*
Left: *On board an army ferry boat going between Staten Island and Manhattan in 1957*
Right: *Reviewing troops in Ghana*
Below: *This five-year-old, in Sierra Leone, has pictures of the Queen printed on her dress*

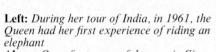

Left: *During her tour of India, in 1961, the Queen had her first experience of riding an elephant*
Above: *One of a troupe of dancers in Sierre Leone, in 1961*
Above right: *In 1961, at Katmandu, capital of the Himalayan kingdom of Nepal*
Oval: *Looking over the Tississat Falls at Lake Tana, Ethiopia, in 1965*
Below: *At the Berlin Wall in 1965 during the Queen's State visit to West Germany*
Below right: *The Queen and Prince Philip reviewing British troops in West Germany during their visit in 1965*

The Queen's money

The Queen is a very wealthy woman in her own right—though not the multi-million-airess that some people imagine she is. Her personal jewellery is, of course, almost priceless, and the royal art collection alone is worth millions. But she holds this in trust for the nation, and it's inconceivable that any of it would ever come on to the open market. However, the Queen does have a huge advantage over others, including members of her own family, in not being liable for either income or transfer tax.

In addition to owning Balmoral and its estate of 80,000 acres, (purchased in the 1850s by Prince Albert for £31,000), and Sandringham, (bought for £220,000), the Queen derives an annual income of some £380,000 from the Duchy of Lancaster—lands and property spread over 52,000 acres of Lancashire and Yorkshire but also including leaseholds in London's City and West End. By law, she pays no tax on this income, nor on her private income from sources such as stocks and shares.

Quite apart from her personal finances, the Queen receives a set amount each year from the Government to cover the cost of the official duties of the Head of State—running the Royal Family "as a firm", to use King George VI's description. This allowance is known as the Civil List.

In 1971, with rising prices affecting the cost of the monarchy like everything else, the Queen placed before Parliament what amounted to a pay claim. "Her Majesty requests that consideration should be given by the House of Commons to the provision for Her Civil List made by Parliament in the first year of her reign. Her Majesty regrets that developments in the intervening years have made that provision inadequate for the maintenance of that standard of service to Her people to which She believes they wish Her and Her family to adhere, and has commanded that papers necessary for a full consideration of the subject shall be laid before the House."

When a Committee looked into the matter it discovered the royal accounts were £240,000 in the red—due mostly to a 16 per cent rise in salaries and wages among the Royal Household since 1952—and that the Queen was using her own money to pay some of these increased expenses.

From January 1, 1972 the Civil List was re-drawn so that the Queen no longer has a Privy Purse—the equivalent to a salary—but a lump sum instead, granted by Parliament to cover Household salaries, pensions, and expenses. This lump sum, which is protected against inflation, rose to £1,665,000 last year.

The Queen provided £118,000 to meet official expenses of those members of her family who are not taken care of by another Government fund called the Consolidated Fund. Last year this Fund paid Prince Philip £85,000, Princess Anne £45,000, the Queen Mother £140,000, Princess Margaret £50,000 and Princess Alice, Duchess of Gloucester, £25,000. Prince Charles receives nothing from the Consolidated Fund, but he does retain half of the revenue from the Duchy of Cornwall, which works out at about £145,000 a year, free of income tax.

The Government pays for the upkeep of royal palaces, with the exception of Balmoral and Sandringham which are private homes, but the Queen pays for her own domestic staff. She also pays for the traditional Palace garden parties, though a ministry is responsible for the upkeep of the gardens. There are many anomalies about what should come out of the taxpayers' pockets and what should rightly be charged to the Queen's personal account. But surely one of the strangest practices occurs on the rare occasions when the Queen attends a Gala at the Royal Opera House in Covent Garden: she takes along her own food!

A rare picture of a royal spending spree— taken in 1935 it shows Princess Elizabeth and Princess Margaret leaving a book shop in Forfar, having bought a few gifts!

One month's engagements

The following is a record of the engagement diary of the Queen and Prince Philip, abridged from the Court Circular, for just one month—June 1976.

1st Returned from Finland aboard Britannia, toured Tilbury docks. Prince Philip opened Harwich Pilot station.

2nd Received Master and Worshipful Company of Gardeners. Attended Epsom Races. Prince Philip gave evening reception for British International Gliding team.

3rd Received Ambassador, Admiral, and General. Prince Philip flew to Birmingham to present Design Council Awards, then flew back to accompany the Queen at reception and dinner at London Zoo. Later he left in royal train for Manchester.

4th Received members of the United States and British Curtis Cup Golf Team. Prince Philip visited University of Salford.

5th Prince Philip took salute at second rehearsal of Queen's Birthday Parade at Horse Guards. In afternoon visited centenary regatta of Model Yacht Sailing Association on the Round Pond, Kensington Gardens.

7th Visited Coldstream Guards barracks at Windsor. Prince Philip attended Trinity House Annual Court and lunched with the Elder Brethren.

8th Received General Haig, Supreme Allied Commander Europe, and Mrs. Haig. In evening, received the Right Hon. James Callaghan, Prime Minister and First Lord of the Treasury. Prince Philip toured parts of the Kennet and Avon Canal, lunched with the British Waterways Board at Newbury, and dined with the Younger Brethren at Trinity House.

9th Attended reception to mark centenary of founding of Mothers Union. Prince Philip inspected new signalling at London Bridge station, and in evening attended charity greyhound meeting at Wimbledon.

10th Received in audience, and attended Beating Retreat ceremony at Horse Guards. Prince Philip presented Amateur Athletic Board trophies at Buckingham Palace.

11th Invested Lord Clark with Order of Merit. Took farewell of Bulgarian Ambassador. Attended Commonwealth Day Observance Service in Westminster Abbey, went to reception at Marlborough House, gave reception at Buckingham Palace to celebrate Duke of Beaufort's 40 years as Master of the Horse. Prince Philip, in addition, presided at inaugural meeting of Fellowship of Engineering.

12th Took the salute at the Queen's Birthday Parade—Trooping the Colour—and then to Windsor to give a lunch party for the President of Israel.

14th Invested the Right Hon. Sir Harold Wilson and Duke of Grafton with Order of Garter and attended Garter service at St. George's Chapel, Windsor.

15th Attended Ascot race meeting.

16th Attended Ascot race meeting.

17th Attended Ascot race meeting.

18th Invested Sir Philip Moore with insignia of Knight Commander of the Royal Victorian Order, then attended Ascot race meeting.

21st Accompanied by Prince Philip, attended test match between England and the West Indies at Lord's cricket ground.

22nd Greeted President and Madame Valery Giscard d'Estaing at start of the French President's state visit to Britain. Gave a state banquet in the evening.

23rd Received new Iranian ambassador, and James Hamilton MP, Vice-Chamberlain of the Household with Address from House of Commons. Invested Lord Hinton with the Order of Merit. Entertained the French President and his wife at Gala performance at Covent Garden Opera House. Earlier, Prince Philip took Prince Edward with him when he visited the Household Cavalry Regiment at Hyde Park barracks.

24th Investitures and receptions, followed by visit from Dame Patti Menzies, and audience with the Prime Minister. Entertained in evening by President and Madame Giscard d'Estaing at banquet at French Embassy.

25th With the French President and his party flew to Edinburgh, visited Royal Scottish Academy, and Palace of Holyroodhouse before the state visit ended. In afternoon Prince Philip presided at Medical and Dental Graduation ceremony and dined at the Medical School.

26th Attended Pensioners' party at Windsor.

28th Attended reception to mark 50th anniversary of Honourable Company of Master Mariners.

29th Entertained to dinner by the Canadian High Commissioner at 12 Upper Brook Street. Earlier Prince Philip attended reception in his honour given by English Speaking Union.

30th Accompanied by Prince Philip, visited Royal Air Force station, Coningsby, Lincolnshire.

Tradition and honour

When Joan, Countess of Salisbury, was dancing with King Edward III on an April night in 1348 her blue garter somehow slipped from her thigh and fell to the floor. Gallantly stooping to pick it up, King Edward glimpsed a few of his courtiers snickering. "*Honi soit qui mal y pense*," reproved the King. "Shame on him who thinks evil of it."

Some 600 years later the Garter ceremony—"the most noble and amiable company of St. George named the Garter"—is performed in the Throne Room at Windsor Castle. It is the oldest Order of Christian chivalry in Britain. "Tie about thy leg, for thy renown," says the Prelate, the Bishop of Winchester, "this most noble Garter." Then, after more admonition and oath-taking, the Queen places the riband and star on the knight elect, and rests the blue velvet mantle and collar across his shoulders.

Later the newly-created knight and his knight companions—the number is limited to 24—process over the Castle courtyard, to the delight of the spectators. Eagerly the crowds press forward to catch what is a rare glimpse of prime ministers, field-marshals, and other prominent figures of the day dressed in magnificent robes and plumed hats and each bearing the large Garter insignia on their left breast.

There are seven Orders of Knighthood: Garter, Thistle, Bath, St. Michael and St. George, Victorian Order, British Empire and Bachelor. In most cases the Prime Minister,

on the recommendation of others, decides who shall be given honours. But the Queen personally awards the Orders of the Garter and the Thistle, as well as the Order of Merit and the Royal Victorian Order.

Investitures are held about 14 times a year—usually in the gold and white State Ballroom at Buckingham Palace. For the 100 or so people being honoured—they come from all walks of life—it is likely to be the most memorable day in their lives. It was King George VI who, realising this, decided that those being honoured should be allowed to bring two guests.

When the honour is a knighthood, a gentleman usher produces a velvet-covered stool which has been used for this purpose since 1910. A ceremonial sword is then handed to the Queen. At her first investiture

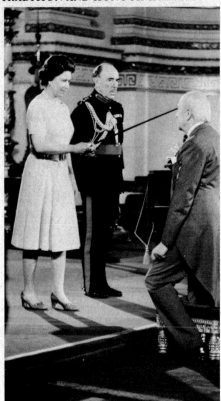

she used the naval sword given to the Duke of Edinburgh by King George VI as a wedding present, but nowadays she uses a lighter one—a Scots Guards sword of her father's.

The new knight kneels, and the Queen taps him lightly on the right, and then the left shoulder. Contrary to what many people imagine, however, she doesn't say "Arise Sir . . ." This was done only on the battle-field when the sovereign needed to learn the name of the soldier before dubbing him.

Above: *The investiture of Sir Cecil Beaton*
Below right: *At Greenwich in 1967, the Queen dubs Sir Francis Chichester after his single-handed voyage around the world using the same sword that Elizabeth I used to knight Sir Francis Drake in 1581*

Royal hobbies

Because the Royal Family is so often photographed at horse-shows and race meetings, many people mistakenly believe that their one interest outside official duties must be horses. But they do, in fact, have many other less publicised hobbies.

The whole family, and in particular the Queen and Prince Philip, are keen on photography and making home movies. And ever since she was a young woman the Queen Mother has loved river fishing—she has spent many happy hours in waders casting for salmon on the waters near Balmoral or close to her home, the Castle of Mey, Caithness, in the north of Scotland.

Prince Charles, too, is an expert fisherman; he joined in a lively correspondence recently with an angling magazine about the do's and don'ts of fly-fishing. And he does, of course, love acting and is himself an excellent mimic.

Although he no longer performs in public, as he did while a student at Cambridge, it doesn't take much to persuade Prince Charles, or the Queen, to join in a game of charades during a weekend at Windsor or while visiting friends. The Prince inherits much of his acting ability from the Queen who, as a child, used to love performing in pantomimes at Windsor.

Prince Philip is not inclined towards acting or the theatre; on the whole, his hobbies are open-air ones. He has loved sailing since he was a boy. And under King George VI's guidance he became an excellent shot—though nowadays he's more concerned with the conservation of wild life than with its careless destruction.

Painting in oils is one of Prince Philip's more relaxing hobbies, and he is especially fond of landscapes.

The two young Princes, Andrew and Edward, are already following the example set by the rest of the family and are each pursuing energetic outdoor hobbies. Prince Andrew, a pupil at Gordonstoun, has been taking gliding lessons with the school Air Training Corps, and both he and his young brother already share their father's love of sailing. In the summer Prince Andrew's aluminium boat, trailer-towed behind a car, is a fairly familiar sight on the roads around Balmoral.

Princess Margaret's wedding

The announcement of Princess Margaret's engagement to a commoner—photographer Antony Armstrong-Jones, who had a studio in London's Pimlico—surprised and delighted everyone. The Queen's younger sister, fourth in line to the Throne at the time, was 29 and many people had waited anxiously for her to find happiness.

On May 6, 1960, it was warm and sunny for the crowds standing eight deep along the wedding route. A huge arch of roses and white banners bearing the intertwined initials of the bride and groom decorated the Mall. Sentimental love songs were played over loud-speakers. Flower girls handed out red carnations to passers-by. Everywhere there was a feeling of romantic carnival.

Inside Westminster Abbey 2,000 guests awaited the ceremony itself. Television cameras, positioned among the guests, were to carry live pictures of a royal wedding into millions of homes for the first time.

Princess Margaret made a spectacular bride—tiny, bright and very beautiful. Her dress, by Norman Hartnell, was of silk organza with a tight bodice and long, close-fitting sleeves. Chief among the eight bridesmaids was Princess Anne, only nine years old.

During the wedding breakfast at Buckingham Palace, a mass of people pressed towards the Palace railings chanting: "We want Margaret . . . We want Tony", and with a frantic rush they broke through the police cordon, cheering and shouting. In the tradition of all royal wedding couples, Princess Margaret and her husband stepped on to the balcony and waved and smiled for several minutes.

In fact, they enjoyed their wedding reception so much they were 25 minutes late in leaving, in an open Rolls-Royce, for their honeymoon aboard the royal yacht Britannia and in the West Indies. As they drove out of the Palace courtyard, wedding guests, family and friends ran after the car throwing confetti and rose petals. Tugs packed with sight-seers cheered them down the Thames as far as Tilbury, and girls of a Sea Rangers unit ran up the flag message: "Good luck, God speed."

Three years later Princess Margaret presented her wedding dress to the London Museum, and the banners in the Mall went on sale for £45 each.

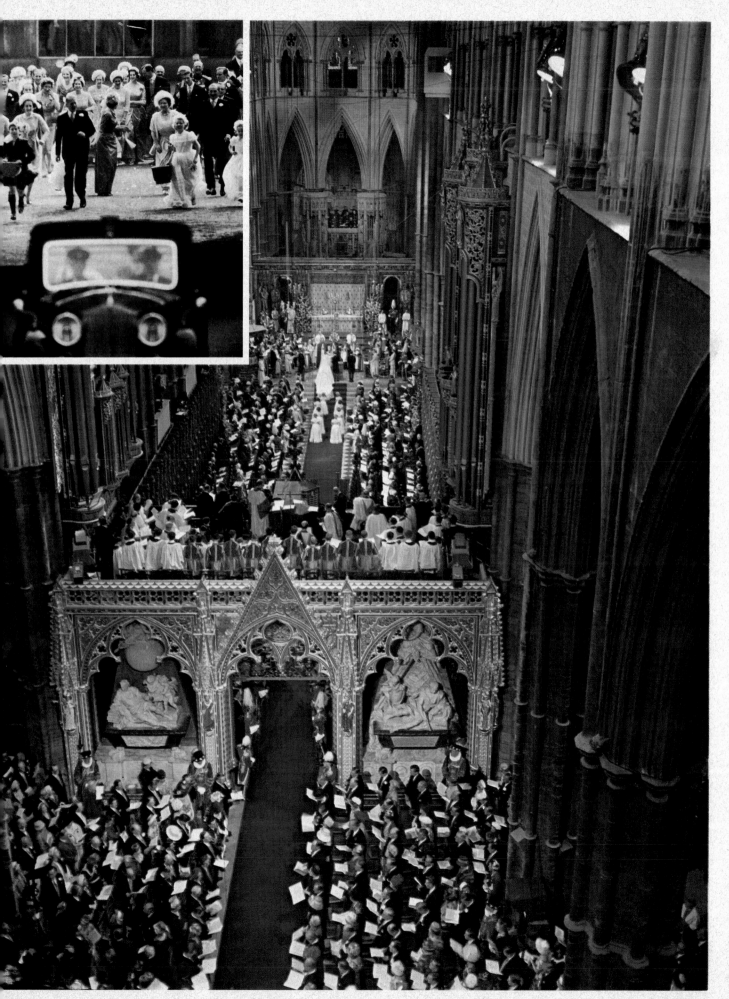

Family christenings

Over the years, royal christenings have become enveloped with family tradition.

Ever since Queen Victoria's second child, Edward, was christened in 1842, successive generations of the Royal Family have used the same christening robe of Honiton lace, worn over a satin petticoat, and the same silver gilt font has been brought from the Gold Pantry at Windsor to wherever the ceremony is taking place. The Queen, her father, and her four children were all christened in the same robe and at the same font with water from the River Jordan. And when Princess Anne was christened another tradition was begun. Sprigs of oak, grown from acorns that had been planted on the Queen's wedding day, were nestled among the flowers around the font.

Although group photographs are sometimes published afterwards, royal christenings tend to be private, family affairs. All but one of the Queen's four children were baptised in the music room at Buckingham Palace, with only relatives and close friends

Above left: *Prince Charles' christening—on the Queen's right is the late Dowager Marchioness of Milford Haven*
Below left: *Princess Anne's christening, in 1950*
Oval: *Prince Edward's first appearance in public, in 1964*
Above: *Lady Sarah Armstrong-Jones, born in 1964*
Far right: *Prince Andrew, born in 1960*
Below right: *Princess Alexandra with 10-week-old James Ogilvy, in 1964*

present. Prince Edward was christened in the private chapel at Windsor Castle and, emphasising the fact that it was a religious and family occasion, there were no group photographs published afterwards.

At Prince Charles' christening, in December 1948, King George VI and the Duke of Edinburgh wore morning-dress while Princess Elizabeth was dressed in a long, red coat and brown hat. White narcissi, Christmas roses and white heather decorated the plinth of the font, and the organist of the Chapels Royal played Handel's Water Music on the piano as the boys of the Chapel Royal choir filed into the room, adding even more vivid colour to the scene with their Tudor uniforms of scarlet and gold.

After the singing of the hymn Holy, Holy, Holy, the Prince's nurse, Sister Helen Rowe, handed the baby to his aunt, Princess Margaret, who in turn placed him in the arms of the Archbishop of Canterbury. It was Princess Margaret who announced in a clear voice the four names of her first nephew: "Charles Philip Arthur George." As an illustration of the economic state of the country at the time, it is worth recalling that on the day before the christening two women officials of the Ministry of Food went to Buckingham Palace and handed in a child's green ration book for the use of Prince Charles!

Sporting Princes

Having a father as energetic as Prince Philip, and being educated at adventure-minded schools such as Gordonstoun, probably makes it hard not to try, at least, to excel in some sport or other.

So far none of the Queen's sons has shown the prowess and the dedication that earned their sister a place in the Montreal Olympics, but nonetheless all three plainly enjoy their various sporting activities.

Prince Charles hunts, shoots and fishes; he also sails, skis and plays polo. And, if you count his flying as a sport, he can pilot a jet, or land a helicopter on a cabbage patch. But he once told an interviewer that one of the few sports he would not like to attempt was rock-climbing. "I don't particularly like the idea of having to cling to a rock-face by my fingernails," he said.

Prince Andrew would probably enjoy doing all the things his elder brother has done. Just turning 17, he already looks like becoming something of a dare-devil. So far we have seen him sailing and booting a rugger ball about. But he has joined Gordonstoun's Air Training Corps, has earned his glider pilot's wings, and it's expected that, in a year or so, he will be learning about powered flight too.

Of the Queen's three sons, Prince Edward is probably the one who's least interested in sport. But perhaps that's because at his age—13 this year—he hasn't yet had a chance to find out which sport he enjoys most. At present he plays football and cricket, and sails with Prince Andrew.

One of the benefits all the Queen's children have enjoyed is tuition from experts. Uffa Fox taught Prince Charles how to sail; Dan Maskell showed Prince Andrew how to play tennis. But all along their greatest spur and inspiration has probably been their father, who is the kind of man who doesn't like to see a child sitting around doing nothing. He has gained so much pleasure himself from physical exertion that he doesn't want others to miss out.

When, in 1971, Prince Philip realised that his own polo-playing days were over because of a damaged wrist, he must have wondered what kind of sport he could turn to next. In fact, with characteristic zest, he was very soon charging around in a carriage drawn by two horses—helping, incidentally, to revive a sport that has since been promoted to Olympic standard.

Above and below: *A man of many energetic sports, Prince Charles also pilots a helicopter—which he finds quite as enjoyable as ski-ing or playing polo. Like his grandmother, the Prince also loves a quiet day's fishing*

Left: *Prince Edward playing football with some of his schoolmates, in February 1970*

Above right: *Prince Charles takes to the sea—Prince Edward enjoys a carriage event, at a horse-show*

Right: *Prince Philip enters into a riotous game of bicycle polo at Windsor in 1967 with his usual zest, but since having to abandon playing proper polo he has taken up driving a carriage and pair with equal success*

Jewels of state

The Crown Jewels of England, guarded in the Tower of London, are almost all of 17th century origin, or later—not nearly so old as most people imagine. For, after the execution of Charles I in 1649, Cromwell's men set about the destruction of regalia, some dating from the early middle ages.

Right: *The Orb and Sceptre—in the Sceptre is a diamond weighing 530 carats*
Below: *The Great Sword of State dating from 1678; the Swords of Justice; and Curtana or the Sword of Mercy*
Below right: *St. Edward's Crown, worn only for the actual ceremony of coronation*

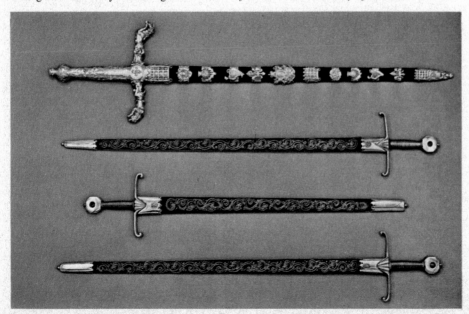

The Ampulla and Anointing Spoon—the oldest objects among the regalia. The golden eagle was probably first used at the coronation of Henry IV

The Queen Mother's Crown. In the cross is the famous Indian diamond, Koh-i-noor, traditionally supposed to bring luck to a woman wearer

The State Crown of Queen Mary, made for the Consort of George V to wear at his coronation in 1911. Among the stones used are the diamonds known as Stars of Africa

The Imperial State Crown. Since Queen Victoria's coronation this is always used by the Sovereign on state occasions. It contains over 3,000 precious stones, mainly diamonds and pearls

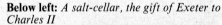

The Coronation Rings—including one made for William IV and another for Queen Victoria—and the Armills, a present from the Commonwealth for the Queen's coronation

The Prince of Wales' Crown, fashioned entirely of gold and dating from 1729

Below left: *A salt-cellar, the gift of Exeter to Charles II*

Jubilees of the past

"Today is the day on which I have reigned longer, by a day, than any English sovereign," wrote Queen Victoria in her dairy on September 23, 1896. In June the following year the "Lady Ruler", as one newspaper proprietor called her, had been Queen for sixty glorious years and the country was to mark her Diamond Jubilee with a jamboree of celebration.

Britain was at the zenith of her Imperial power and, even though there was terrible poverty and cruel inequality in parts of the country, the vast majority of people saw in their 78-year-old Queen a symbol of Britain's greatness. When she drove through the streets of London in an open coach drawn by six greys, on her way to a thanksgiving service at St. Paul's Cathedral, thousands of her subjects not only lined the streets and leaned out of windows but banked themselves in tiers on roof-tops as well. "She Wrought Her People Lasting Good", proclaimed a banner at the Bank of England, and few would have disagreed.

Queen Victoria herself, wearing black and holding a small, white silk parasol, was deeply moved by the reception. "None ever, I believe, has met with such an ovation as was given to me, passing through those six miles of streets. The crowds were quite indescribable, and their enthusiasm truly marvellous and deeply touching. The cheering was quite deafening, and every face seemed to be filled with real joy."

In 1977, it is quite within the realms of possibility that the Queen too will reign at least as long as her great-great-grandmother

and the country will celebrate another royal diamond jubilee in the year 2012.

Naturally, diamond jubilees are rare, but comparatively few British monarchs have reigned even as long as 25 years—only 14 since 1100. After Queen Victoria's Diamond Jubilee there was a 38-year gap before the next Silver Jubilee, of King George V, in 1935. He was a very popular king—just how

Above: *King George V and Queen Mary drive through London's East End during the Silver Jubilee celebrations of 1935*
Below: *A painting of Queen Victoria arriving at St. Paul's Cathedral for a Diamond Jubilee service in 1897*
Right: *English monarchs, up to Queen Victoria's time, who have reigned 25 years and more*

THE ENGLISH MONARCHS WHO REIGNED 25 YEARS:

JUBILEE PREDECESSORS OF H.M. KING GEORGE V.

HENRY I., 1100-1135: A DETAIL FROM AN OLD ENGRAVING BY G. VERTUE.

HENRY III., 1216-1272: DETAIL FROM AN ELECTROTYPE IN THE NATIONAL PORTRAIT GALLERY FROM THE EFFIGY BY W. TOREL.

HENRY II., 1154-1189: DETAIL FROM A PRINT FROM HIS MONUMENTAL EFFIGY AT FONTEVRAUD.

EDWARD I., 1272-1307: DETAIL OF A PRINT FROM AN ANCIENT STATUE OF THE KING AT CARNARVON CASTLE.

EDWARD III., 1327-1377: DETAIL FROM AN ELECTROTYPE IN THE NATIONAL PORTRAIT GALLERY FROM THE EFFIGY IN THE ABBEY.

HENRY VI., 1422-1461: DETAIL FROM A PAINTING BY AN UNKNOWN ARTIST IN THE NATIONAL PORTRAIT GALLERY.

HENRY VIII., 1509-1547: DETAIL FROM A PAINTING, PERHAPS BY LUKE HORNEBOLT, IN THE NATIONAL PORTRAIT GALLERY.

VICTORIA, 1837-1901: DETAIL FROM THE PAINTING BY BENJAMIN CONSTANT.

CHARLES II., 1660-1685: DETAIL FROM A PAINTING BY AN UNKNOWN ARTIST IN THE NATIONAL PORTRAIT GALLERY.

GEORGE II., 1727-1760: DETAIL FROM A PAINTING BY THOMAS HUDSON IN THE NATIONAL PORTRAIT GALLERY.

ELIZABETH, 1558-1603: DETAIL FROM A PAINTING BY AN UNKNOWN ARTIST IN THE NATIONAL PORTRAIT GALLERY.

GEORGE III., 1760-1820: DETAIL FROM A PAINTING (STUDIO OF ALLAN RAMSAY) IN THE NATIONAL PORTRAIT GALLERY.

popular he himself didn't realise until he'd driven through London's East End streets and saw them bedecked with Union Jacks and lined with cloth-capped workers who ran after his Daimler shouting good luck messages. "I'd no idea they felt like that about me," he remarked as he arrived back at Buckingham Palace. "I am beginning to think they must really like me for myself."

The wireless, more than anything, brought the King to the people. Until he made the first royal broadcast, in 1924, the mass of people had never heard a king or queen speak. The King's voice was warm, vibrant, and his choice of words, spoken slowly and clearly, held a kind of mesmerism. At the end of an exhausting day of Jubilee celebrations on May 6, 1935 he broadcast a message of thanks "to my people everywhere". He continued in words that middle-aged men and women still remember vividly today, almost 42 years later: "I am speaking to the children above all. Remember children, the King is speaking to *you*." It was magic.

Above: *The Royal Family on the balcony at Buckingham Palace after King George V's Silver Jubilee celebrations in 1935. Princess Elizabeth has her chin in her hands*
Right: *Queen Victoria entering the City of London on her Diamond Jubilee in 1897*

A health unto Her Majesty

Fortunately the Queen has never had a serious illness in her life. She possesses a strong physique, though it has been over-taxed at times—particularly during the early part of her reign when her sense of duty tended to override her doctors' well-intentioned advice.

In 1958 she battled against streaming eyes and cold to undertake a tour of Scotland and the north of England. But eventually she had to succumb and, only an hour before she was due to start a visit to Carlisle, the royal train was sent to bring her back to London. It was six weeks before she was able to undertake any other public engagements.

Catarrh and sinusitis are the twin troubles which plague the Queen most often. She has always been prone to colds and laryngitis but hates to disappoint people who have been looking forward to seeing her. She is not one to make use of the diplomatic illness. When she has a cold, she really does have a cold—and it's usually a bad one.

Altogether there are 25 men—and one woman—who can officially call themselves physician, surgeon or dentist to the Queen. Naturally the list includes some of the most distinguished specialists in the medical profession. But the doctors she sees most are the five "apothecaries to the Household"—her family doctors at Buckingham Palace, Windsor, Sandringham, Holyroodhouse and Balmoral.

In January 1969 a woman doctor was added to the Queen's list of physicians for the first time. What was more remarkable was that Dr. Margery Grace Blackie, holder of an impressive number of qualifications, is a homoeopathic physician. She therefore uses treatments based on the theory that diseases are curable with the use of minute quantities of drugs which produce effects similar to the symptoms of the disease itself. Dr. Blackie is also Dean of the Faculty of Homoeopathy at the Royal London Homoeopathic Hospital.

Now in her sixties and living in Kensington, it is reported that Dr. Blackie has attended the Queen on a number of occasions, presumably using homoeopathic treatment.

In the early part of the Queen's reign her doctors—as well as other advisers—were concerned that she might totally exhaust herself with her heavy load of engagements, both in Britain and abroad. There were calls for a curtailment, which went almost unheeded.

But since the nineteen-sixties—from about the time of Prince Edward's arrival—the Queen does seem to have learned to pace herself more, so that she can withstand hours of walking and handshaking, and weeks of jet travel between continents, without showing any sign of tiredness.

Even so, only a remarkably fit and relaxed woman could work as hard as the Queen obviously does.

Above: *When she visited the State Museum in Amsterdam in March 1958 the Queen was beginning to show the strain that was to be followed later by a recurrence of heavy colds and catarrh*

Below: *Dr. Margery Grace Blackie, the first woman to be appointed a physician to the Queen. Here she is pictured at her country home, Hedingham Castle, in Essex*

Right: *Dr. Richard Bayliss, one of the Queen's physicians. He attended Princess Anne after her riding accident in 1976*

On canvas...

There is a Poet Laureate and a Master of the Queen's Musick, but there is no equivalent position in art—no Royal Portrait Painter. So each year the Queen sits for as many artists who wish to paint her portrait as time will allow. Usually the paintings have been commissioned either by army regiments who are proud to have the Queen as their Colonel-in-Chief, or by one of the ancient Companies of Craftsmen in the City of London.

Of the scores of portraits of the Queen that have been painted in the past 25 years probably the two best known are both the work of the Italian painter Pietro Annigoni. The one showing the Queen in the Robes of the Garter (far right) was painted in 1955 and most people seemed to approve when it was hung in the Royal Academy, though some have always thought it too "chocolate-boxy". It was commissioned at a fee of £2,000 by the Company of Fishmongers, and Annigoni worked on it for four months, being given a total of 12 sittings by the Queen in the yellow drawing-room at Buckingham Palace. Afterwards Annigoni explained: "I tried to show her not simply with the regal dignity of a Queen but also as she appeared to me—as a beautiful young woman."

Fifteen years later, when the Queen was 44, Annigoni returned to England to paint the other portrait shown on the right. This time it was commissioned by the National Portrait Gallery, and this time Annigoni came in for some criticism from those who thought it made the Queen look very unhappy. He replied to his critics: "I didn't want to paint her sad, but I didn't want to paint her as a film star. The monarch is in the robe, and the woman is in the face—simple, undistracted by any decoration."

In contrast the painting below, by Michael Noakes was specially commissioned to celebrate the Silver Jubilee and the Centenary of Manchester Town Hall, where it now hangs.

...and through lens

Being a keen amateur photographer herself the Queen is particularly interested in the work of professional photographers.

On the right is one of Sir Cecil Beaton's famous portraits of the Queen. This one shows her in the Robes of the Order of the Garter with the outline of Windsor Castle and St. George's Chapel in the background.

The photograph below is a study by Karsh of Ottowa, Canada, taken early on in the Queen's reign.

And at the foot of the page is another portrait by Cecil Beaton, taken of the young Princess Elizabeth before her accession to the Throne.

This dramatic portrait of the Queen was photographed by Sir Cecil Beaton and was first shown in the National Portrait Gallery Exhibition of 1968—the first such exhibition to be devoted to the work of a single camera artist.
On the left are Cecil Beaton's portrait to mark the Queen's 43rd birthday (top), and two of Peter Grugeon's informal portraits of the Queen, taken at Windsor Castle in 1975

25 years of royal fashion

To say that the Queen isn't interested in fashion simply isn't true. Although not a dedicated fashion follower she does enjoy a style of her own, at the same time conforming to certain expectations and restrictions.

As a young woman she favoured styles which showed off a trim waist—princess-line frocks with very full, calf-length skirts.

Her hair, more softly waved than today, suited the head-hugging caps and half-hats which were usually made with flowers and feathers. Her hand-bags were the soft, pouch type, and she liked peep-toe sandals.

For a while she kept to the wartime style of knee-length pleated skirts, blousey tops and padded shoulders. These suited her particularly well and when she did eventually change in favour of "The New Look" it

was rather later than most other fashion-conscious women.

Her evening dresses during the Fifties were mostly of the crinoline variety which suited a small-waisted figure, and many had thin shoulder straps or off-the-shoulder flounces. Less heavily embroidered than her later dresses their impact relied on layer upon layer of pastel-coloured nets and tulles. (The famous "biscuit tin" picture of the Queen in a regal blue tulle dress —with Prince Philip in naval uniform—is a good example.)

Around this time she often wore a mink coat—made by her furriers, Calman Links—which she still has in her wardrobe, though it is rarely seen these days. For informal occasions, the Queen wore tweed suits with nipped-in waists and pleated skirts—not unlike her grey honeymoon suit which, it is said, still fits her.

While British fashion took on an air of excitement in the Sixties the Queen, still patronising Norman Hartnell and Hardy Amies, stayed with the more matronly styles of the previous decade. But clothes were becoming more informal and the elaborate silk and chiffon coat and dress ensembles now seemed a little out of place.

By the time the Sixties were drawing to a close, however, the Queen had obviously reconsidered and—whether it was her own wishes or Mr. Hartnell's which prevailed—the choice of colours improved, with strong vibrant shades replacing the insipid pastels. Simple, well-tailored, unfussy coats and suits began to appear. The shiny satins and silks vanished for daytime to be replaced with prettier wools, linens and matt silks. Out went the crinolines

Members of the Royal Family often choose bright colours so they can be spotted among the crowd. Rarely is the Queen seen in creased clothes, even after many hours of travel. This is because, while the styles are simple, the fabrics are top quality—good wools, silks with firm linings, rarely any man-made fibres. She keeps her clothes for several seasons, frequently returning them to the couturiers for running repairs and alterations.

What happens to the Queen's clothes when she can no longer wear them remains something of an official secret, but it is thought that she gives them to members of her household

and a new, beautifully elegant Queen arrived at Gala occasions wearing mostly sheath dresses—lots of white, heavily beaded with silvers and golds, topped by a glamorous fox fur. Suddenly she looked taller and slimmer than ever before.

She began to appear at evening engagements without a tiara, her hair more bouffant.

The Queen's shoes, made by Rayne, haven't changed to any great extent—she still favours unfussy pumps in black, brown, navy or white for day, silver or gold at night.

Her hats, too, began to have a sense of fun—pleats, scarf-styles, drapes, floppy berets and colourful bretons appeared. And instead of simply complementing the colour of her coat or dress, they were often in matching fabrics or trimmed to match the lining of her outfit. Her new milliner, Simone Mirman, must take most of the credit for these refreshing new styles.

By 1970, the Queen had shown that she could wear the most up-to-the-minute styles with the necessary panache. She'd wowed the Canadians with an elegant trouser suit and a bright red satin evening suit with its tailored jacket and slim, ankle-length skirt.

Her Seventies look is quite different to that of the tailored Sixties. She now has a new designer, Ian Thomas—who is Hartnell trained but has ideas of his own—and he's persuaded her to wear the unstructured styles, relaxed and less dominating. He's even put her into floppy culottes for some of her entertaining at home.

When she went to America for the bicentennial celebrations, her clothes—by Hartnell, Amies and Thomas—highlighted the Queen of the second half of the Seventies. A pretty navy and white tiger-striped dress, a flowing chiffon caped dress in lilac, a fitted linen suit with short sleeves, were all worn with largish, wide-brimmed hats. Her evening gowns were strong-coloured chiffons except for the glorious dress she wore in Washington—her favourite silvery white, it had its own cape, embroidered to match, and a skirt slit to the knee.

She deals with the rain practically, with a cape—either natural-coloured or the bright yellow silk one she's had for years. Another favourite cape is the one made by Gieves and Hawkes in navy wool barathea—worn in a famous portrait by Cecil Beaton—which she bought nearly 10 years ago.

Quite often the same outfits re-appear—she wore the blue silk coat she'd had made for

Wherever she goes the Queen's clothes are personally attended to by Miss Margaret "Bobo" McDonald, who plans the Queen's outfit for the following day, assembles the correct jewellery and accessories, and lays them all out next morning.

Officially titled the Queen's Dresser, she arranges for the various British couturiers who design for the Queen—Norman Hartnell, Hardy Amies and Ian Thomas—to come to the Palace for long fitting sessions. The Queen has been known to turn down a tour design "because Miss McDonald says it won't travel well".

Seldom photographed, Bobo McDonald holds a very special place among the Palace staff and must know the Queen better than any person outside the Royal Family

Knowing that she is going to
be photographed from every
angle and in every light, the
Queen's designers select prints
with great care. Wild stripes
and heavy geometrics can
create some strange illusions,
and the unrelieved sludgy
colours, though becoming
in real life, can look
extremely ageing, and drab,
in a photograph.

People organising an event
the Queen is to attend often
worry that the colours of the
bouquet they are to present
to her will clash with the
colour of her outfit. But
a phone call to the Palace
will reassure them that there
are very few flower colours
that would, in fact, clash
violently with the primary
tones preferred by the
Queen

Princess Anne's wedding for the State Opening of Parliament the following autumn, and there's an old seven-eighths coat that's seen well over 10 years of country outings.

All her clothes are sketched by the designer to a standard size and are kept in book form. The Queen flicks through the book and selects her outfits then Margaret "Bobo" McDonald, her ex-nanny and now her personal and trusted attendant, sees to the rest.

The Queen is happiest when she's in the country, relaxed, in unfashionable boots, wellingtons or serviceable walking shoes. At Balmoral she wears a kilted skirt and suede or tweed jacket, or a tweed suit or coat, and if not bareheaded, she simply wears a headscarf.

On other informal occasions the Queen is often still in the public gaze, like at the Braemar Games, the Badminton Horse Trials or when presenting prizes at horse-shows. For these engagements she's often bareheaded these days, wearing a simple Chanel-type suit, or afternoon dress.

But even when she does dress more casually it is clear to see that her choice has been carefully considered. For instance, at the Braemar Games in 1961, she wore a camel coat with featherplumed beret. Fourteen years later she chose a soft green, raglan coat, overchecked in white, and a floppy green and white beret. Each outfit a perfect choice for the occasion.

Before she departs on any of her tours, there's always one request to Simone Mirman—that she make a blue turban, a special favourite of the Queen.

Her Majesty's hats, in which she is said to take great interest, have to be off the face so she can be seen from many angles. A replica of the Queen's head, known as a "dolly", is kept at her milliner's—either Aage Thaarup or Simone Mirman.

Even though hats are not now the general fashion they once were, the ladies of the Royal Family rarely appear without them on formal occasions. Apart from other considerations, as Princess Anne has explained, they do away with the need for constant attention to hair-do's.

The Queen is constantly introducing new outfits into her wardrobe and may earmark a particular design for a foreign tour as much as a year in advance. Her shoes—plain for day, with medium heels—are made by Rayne but she has very few pairs of evening shoes, perhaps one pair of gold, one pair of silver

Prince Charles' house

When renovations are completed, Chevening House, near Chipstead in Kent, will become Prince Charles' first private home. Designed by Inigo Jones, the house was bought by the Stanhope family in 1717 for £28,000. For 250 years its ownership remained with the family. But when the 7th Earl of Stanhope, a former Cabinet Minister, died without direct heirs in 1967, he bequeathed the house and its 3,500 acres of parkland and farms to the nation. It was his wish that they should be put to the use of prime ministers or a member of the Royal Family, and he left a trust fund of £250,000 to help with running costs.

The Queen went to look at the house privately the following year, and work on restoring it began later. But by 1973 there was still no official word about its future, except that a Buckingham Palace spokesman said: "Prince Charles will definitely not take it and, as far as we know, neither will any other member of the Royal Family."

Then, in May 1974, the Prime Minister told a surprised and delighted House of Commons that the heir to the Throne would move into the house as soon as the renovation and redecorating were finished.

Chevening is about an hour's drive from central London and Prince Charles has been down to the house from time to time to see how work is progressing. Now and again rumours leak out—like the news that the Prince had chosen a colour scheme of blue and white for his own bathroom—but a 20-ft.-high wall and the removal of some road signs in the locality discourage many of the inquisitive sight-seers.

The house has 83 rooms altogether but is divided into three distinct parts. One wing houses a large library, and another will be used mainly by staff. The main house has four bedrooms and bathrooms on the ground floor as well as the principle reception rooms and a fully-modernised kitchen. A beautiful staircase in Spanish oak leads up to the six bedrooms and four bathrooms on the next floor.

Surrounding the house are acres of lawns, where Prince Charles has been happy to allow village fetes and fairs to take place. The grounds also include some fine specimen trees, and lakes which have recently been restocked with ducks and Canada geese.

When all the plans have been carried out, Chevening will be as handsome as ever it was, if not more so. A house fit for a Prince, indeed.

Princess Anne's new home

Princess Anne and her husband Captain Mark Phillips looked at several houses before it was announced in July last year that the Queen had bought them the magnificent Gatcombe Park in Gloucestershire. The price paid was variously reported as being between £425,000 and £725,000.

The stone-built mansion, built about 1760, had previously belonged to Lord Butler, Master of Trinity College, Cambridge, who inherited it from his father-in-law, Samuel Courtauld, the textile magnate. It stands in 750 acres, two-thirds of which is prime farmland, the rest being woodland. The town of Stroud lies five miles to the south and Captain Phillips' parents' home is just 20 miles away, in Wiltshire.

Princess Anne and her husband intend to continue running the estate as a farming enterprise with a beef-breeding herd of 190 cattle, and main crops of wheat and barley.

The house itself needed a great deal of renovation before it was ready for the couple to move into it. The kitchen was antiquated, and the four reception rooms and five main bedrooms, though handsomely proportioned and furnished, required redecorating. But even at first glance Gatcombe Park is the kind of house that dreams are made of. Sweeping lawns, a magnificent and huge conservatory, white shutters to the windows, and roses, jasmine, and wistaria clinging to the walls. There are plenty of stables for the horses, and even a lake with a boathouse for still summer evenings.

Living at Gatcombe Park will be a big change from Oak Grove, at Sandhurst, which was the couple's first home after their marriage in 1973. Rented army accommodation at £8 a week, the house was renovated at a cost of £25,000, but even then it appeared somewhat unattractive from the outside. Oak Grove was built between 1810 and 1812, for the Sandhurst Paymaster of the time.

Princess Anne's new home has nothing of the military about it. It is elegance supreme, a perfect place for a young married couple with a love of the country, an ideal home in which to start a family.

Far left: *The boathouse and lake, which form such a picturesque part of the grounds*

Left: *Geoffrey Stevens—who has been farm manager at Gatcombe Park for the past 13 years—with his wife Mary*

Lower pictures *(left to right): The stable-block before renovation; inside the conservatory; and the hall and drawing-room as they were when the Queen first bought the house*

Trooping
the Colour

Trooping the Colour is one of those traditional ceremonies with origins which stretch back over many years. Until about 200 years ago a regiment's flag was the soldiers' rallying point in the smoke and confusion of pitched battle; it was therefore paraded in front of the troops at the end of each day so they would know exactly what it looked like. Gradually the Colour—never called a flag—came to represent the very spirit of the regiment and not merely a form of identification.

Each regiment has two Colours—the Queen's and the Regimental—and since 1805 battalions have taken it in turn to troop their Colour before the Sovereign in an annual ceremony.

In Queen Victoria's reign the ceremony was used to celebrate her birthday, in May. Nowadays it is held on the Sovereign's official birthday, a Saturday early in June, when London is full of holiday-makers.

The 62 officers and 1,500 guardsmen who perform the ceremony drill daily for six weeks in preparation. And the Queen herself practises riding side-saddle for several hours.

Then on the day itself, escorted by her Household Cavalry, she rides out from Buckingham Palace and up the Mall to Horse Guards Parade—a vast expanse of asphalt where the Royal Palace of Whitehall stood until 1698. Everything down to the smallest detail is planned for her to arrive on the parade ground on the stroke of 11.

Trooping the Colour is one of the most impressive ceremonies in the royal calendar. With the music of the massed bands echoing across the green of St. James's Park, the crunching stamp of the soldiers' boots, and the sergeant majors' yells of command reaching to the gates of Buckingham Palace itself, it has always excited onlookers—including the Queen's children.

When Prince Charles was five the Queen Mother and Princess Margaret took him and his sister to watch the ceremony in an open landau. And in 1965, after she'd returned to the Palace, the Queen—still wearing her ceremonial uniform—stepped out on to the balcony to watch the traditional RAF fly-past holding Prince Andrew by one hand, and cradling the baby Prince Edward in her other arm.

Even the Russians were impressed when the ceremony was shown on their television in 1960—the first live transmission from Britain to Russia. They commented to a reporter on the precision of the soldiers' drill, and told him how slim they thought the Queen looked . . . ►

Above: *The Queen riding Doctor, the police horse, at the 1963 ceremony*

Left: *Almost unrecognisable under their huge bearskins, Prince Philip with Prince Charles on his left*

Below: *Accompanying Her Majesty at the 1972 ceremony were Prince Philip, and the Duke of Kent (on the dapple grey horse)*

Top right: *The fly-past of the Royal Air Force follows the Trooping the Colour as a tribute to the Queen on her official birthday*

Smiling in the rain

Wherever she goes, the Queen has a reputation of taking the rain with her, just as Queen Victoria was said to bring out the sun. Neither reputation, of course, has much basis. But people are unlikely ever to forget the day the Queen, or any member of the Royal Family, came to visit their town, factory, or school. And if they've stood waiting for hours in the rain they will remember the day even more.

Rain or shine, the Queen's attitude doesn't seem to change. She always has a smile for everyone. In fact it is the Queen's smile and her beautiful complexion that most people remark on after that fleeting moment when the royal car goes by, or the Queen walks just a few feet away.

Royal visits are mooted about a year in advance, and in the following months preparations are made with scrupulous attention to detail. A suggested programme is sent to the Palace but rarely are changes made—except, perhaps, some advice given on timing and security.

The local council holds committee meetings to decide who shall and who shall not be presented to Her Majesty. The local police plan the royal route with meticulous care. And even when Buckingham Palace suggests that expense should be kept to an absolute minimum, and day-to-day life should be disrupted as little as possible, some local authorities will still go to extraordinary lengths to show off their town at its sparkling best.

Tales of "Gentlemen" signs being covered up so they don't appear in photographs are legend. So, too, are accounts of rubbish tips being cleared, and whole buildings being repainted—just for the 30 seconds that it takes for a procession of royal cars to pass by.

Nobody approves of wasting money, but it's not every day a town has a royal visit. And, sometimes as a result, things do get done that might otherwise go neglected for years . . .

When the Queen sailed down the Thames to Reading, in the autumn of 1974, the rain fairly bucketed down. But the crowds who had waited patiently for hours didn't allow the weather to dampen their spirits. And the Queen just put up her umbrella, ignored the puddles, and kept on smiling.

On the right, Prince Philip finds a downpour in Australia during a garden party in Sydney, and the Queen ploughs through the mud at the Badminton Horse Trials in 1959. The sight that made the Queen double up with laughter, above, was seeing a line of army recruits scuttling down ropes, in the rain

A royal wedding in York

York Minster had not witnessed a royal wedding since the marriage of Edward III, in 1328. But Katharine Worsley—a descendant of Oliver Cromwell—was, after all, very much a Yorkshire lass and her bridegroom, the 25-year-old Duke of Kent, had a reputation for breaking with tradition.

For their wedding on June 8, 1961 he had sought, and been granted, permission to wear the magnificent scarlet and blue ceremonial dress of the Royal Scots Greys, complete with busby, which had not been worn since the end of the first world war.

The bride's gown, designed by John Cavanagh, was made of 237 yards of gossamer, silver-woven, white silk gauze. It had no embroidery, no jewels, nor sequins and its sheer simplicity made a striking contrast with the rich splendour of the 27 foreign princes and princesses who came to the wedding.

The Duke was in the army—no. 443787—when he first met Katharine. Her father, Sir William Worsley (who was Lord Lieutenant of the North Riding of Yorkshire) had invited him to visit their home, Hovingham Hall, as a courtesy to the Royal Family. And

the Duke appears to have been captivated by Sir William's daughter almost immediately.

After the marriage ceremony, the newly-weds drove the 23 miles to Hovingham Hall for the reception, slowing down as they travelled to wave to picnickers along the country lanes.

Awaiting them at the reception was a splendid five-tier wedding cake which stood 5 ft. high and weighed 180 lb.—the Duke then experienced some difficulty in cutting through the thick layers of icing with his regimental sword.

As the couple set out for the airport—they were leaving for a honeymoon at Birkhall, near Balmoral—everyone, including the Queen, showered them with rose petals. And all along the route the joyous send-off was repeated with flowers and confetti.

At the airport they boarded the red Heron of the Queen's Flight to find three bottles of champagne and smoked salmon sandwiches had been provided with the compliments of the Queen.

Everyone agreed that it was one of the friendliest royal weddings they had ever seen.

Princess Alexandra, a favourite bride

The announcement that Princess Alexandra was to marry the Honourable Angus Ogilvy took many people by surprise. The newspapers had tipped Lord O'Neill, an Irish peer who owned land in Scotland. Nevertheless, everyone was delighted with the news. Like her mother, Princess Marina, the young Princess had always been a special favourite with the public.

Princess Marina made the announcement on November 30, 1962—28 years to the day after her own wedding to the late Duke of Kent. The handsome Angus Ogilvy was the second son of the 12th Earl of Airlie—a Scotsman who was happiest when tramping the hills, but who worked in the City of London.

The wedding in Westminster Abbey, on April 24, 1963, was attended by 12 members of royal families from abroad. Princess Anne, chief bridesmaid at 12, wore her hair up for the first time in public and looked very grown up. The five bridesmaids wore simple little dresses of heavy white silk with white satin bandeaux in their hair. The two charming little pages—Simon Hay and the five-year-old Master of Ogilvy—were dressed in kilts.

Princess Alexandra was a beautifully elegant bride. She had chosen a magnolia dress in fine cotton lace of acorn and leaf design, with a high round neckline. Matching lace was used for her veil, held in place by the same diamond fringe tiara that her mother had worn as a bride in 1934.

After the wedding 500 guests toasted the bride and groom in the State Apartments of St. James's Palace. They included tenants and staff of Kensington Palace, Coppins (the Kents' home in Buckinghamshire) and Cortachy Castle, the Airlies' ancestral home in Scotland.

As they left for their honeymoon at Birkhall, one baby's red shoe and a tartan ribbon trailed behind their Rolls-Royce.

If they were among the happiest people in Britain that day, surely one of the unluckiest was the bridegroom's niece, Jane Ogilvy. She had contracted measles a few days earlier and, instead of going to the Abbey, she had to content herself with watching the wedding on television.

The Young Princes

The Queen's youngest sons, Prince Andrew and Prince Edward, have been like a second family to her and Prince Philip. Sixteen years separate Prince Edward from Prince Charles. And though Prince Andrew, who is 17 this year, looks very grown up, he is 12 years younger than the heir to the Throne.

But the age difference has in no way spoiled the relationship between the two young Princes and their older brother and sister, because they all share a strong feeling of being a very close family. Prince Charles, in particular, keeps a watchful and affectionate eye on his two young brothers.

Prince Andrew was born on February 19, 1960 at Buckingham Palace—the first baby to be born to a reigning sovereign in 103 years. (The last to have this distinction was Princess Beatrice, the ninth and last child of Queen Victoria.)

From very early on, Prince Andrew showed signs of growing into the most forthright and extrovert of all the royal children. (Once, when asked how old he was, he replied: "Three and a big bit.") And, as

an exuberant and mischievous youngster, he had a knack of getting his own way. "I'm afraid," said his mother at one stage, "that Andrew is no little ray of sunshine." At two he was having riding lessons in the Palace Mews, by the age of four he was going to weekly gym classes, and at seven he was the owner of a £4,000 toy version of James Bond's Aston Martin—which the Queen let him use only at weekends.

In the four years since he left Heatherdown preparatory school, near Ascot, for the greater rigours of Gordonstoun—and the two terms he is spending at Lakefield College School in Canada—Prince Andrew has found more scope for his energies.

When they were small both the young Princes were deliberately kept out of the public gaze. But gradually Prince Andrew is being introduced to his duties as a grown-up member of the Royal Family and—in some ways even more important—to his responsibilities as second in line to the Throne.

So far, Prince Edward seems to be the quiet one of the family—or maybe it's just

that he cannot see any point in trying to compete with the boisterous activities of his brothers and sister, Prince Andrew in particular. He has his father's blond hair, and an altogether more gentle look in his eyes than any of the Queen's other children. His cousin, Lady Sarah Armstrong-Jones, and James Ogilvy, Princess Alexandra's son, have been two of his best friends since they all began taking school classes together.

The Queen has always wished that her children, especially the youngest, should be allowed to grow up and make friends, with as little attention from the public as possible. Their father agrees with her. But as Prince Philip once said: "If you're going to have a monarchy you have got to have a family, and the family's got to be in the public eye."

Prince Edward certainly let it be known that, because his school term hadn't ended, he was the only member of the Royal Family unable to go to the Olympic Games last year. He apparently pestered everyone so much that Prince Charles finally interceded and took him to Montreal himself.

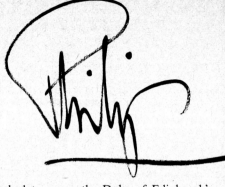

Asked to assess the Duke of Edinburgh's character, Dr. Kurt Hahn, who was his headmaster at Gordonstoun, wrote: "Prince Philip is a born leader, but will need the exacting demands of a great service to do justice to himself. His best is outstanding; his second best is not good enough."

Looking back over the past 25 years it's difficult to see when he was ever at second best. Most people think he has made an outstandingly good Consort to the Queen. Some only feel sorry that his position has prevented him possibly speaking out even more than he has on national topics, or playing more of an executive role in public affairs.

Prince Philip had always hoped to continue his career in the Royal Navy after his marriage to Princess Elizabeth and, but for the untimely illness of King George VI, he might have done so.

As Consort he was never to share in matters of state in quite the same way that the Queen's great-great-grandfather, Prince Albert, had done. But over the years he has given unstinting support to the Queen in other ways, complementing her whenever they appear together in public and giving her advice and encouragement when most needed. In areas where the Queen's natural interest might not have been so great—in industry and science for example—Prince Philip has made it his business to be particularly aware of what's going on.

A man of boundless energy with a somewhat caustic wit, his popularity has remained undiminished. Even now that he is in his fifties it is doubtful that he has mellowed very much.

In public he is the first subject of the Queen, but in private he is the father of a family—it was to him that Captain Mark Phillips went to ask for the hand of Princess Anne. His influence on Prince Charles is unmistakable, though he too is now as independent-minded as his father.

Prince Philip has always been a man who has to be busy about something. And with the restrictions of being Consort he might have occupied himself mainly with sport and pleasure. Instead, over the past 25 years, he has channelled his energy and quick intelligence into several national schemes that help people to help themselves. Altogether he is involved with almost 400 different organisations, the best-known being The Duke of Edinburgh Award scheme which he conceived and pioneered.

He is also President of the National Playing Fields Association. And, as the chairman of the organising committee he did much to launch the annual Queen's Awards to Industry.

Indeed Prince Philip may sometimes feel he had not done as much as he would like to have done, but few would argue with the fact that he has already achieved a great deal.

Top left: *In Kuala Lumpur, 1972, Prince Philip makes friends with an orang-utan*
Top right: *Downing a pint at Cirencester during the National Carriage Championships in 1975*
Left: *Examining a prototype electric bicycle*
Above: *Visiting the London Federation of Boys' Clubs training centre near Amersham*
Below: *With Sir Peter Scott at the Slimbridge Wildfowl Trust*

Ballgowns and banquets

Whenever and wherever the Queen attends a banquet or a ball she steps out of her limousine to a subdued chorus of "oohs" and "aahs" from admiring onlookers. "Isn't she lovely?" they whisper.

Although she isn't tall—just 5 ft. 4 in.—the Queen is an imposing figure, while at the same time her warm, friendly smile always gives people the feeling she has come to see each of them personally.

These pictures were taken over a period of more than 20 years—the one of her dancing goes back as far as 1951—and yet, just looking at them, it's hard to guess when they were taken because age has altered the Queen's appearance so little.

Above: *The Queen addressing the centenary banquet of the TUC at London's Guildhall in 1968*
Oval: *In Japan in 1975 the Queen uses chop-sticks*
Below: *The oriental splendour of a banquet in Malaysia in 1972*
Far left: *Glasses are raised during a state banquet in Mexico in 1975*

and picnics

Although they have to live in London most of the time, at heart the Royal Family are really country-lovers. The Queen, especially, rarely looks more content than when she's tramping across fields or sitting on the bare ground wrapped up in warm coat and headscarf. She loves attending horse-shows and cross-country events with her family and friends, discussing the chances of various horses and riders and then, at the end, presenting the various cups and rosettes.

Picnics of any sort are also a firm favourite. The Queen and Prince Philip look forward to the chance of having the whole family together and setting out, with the dogs, for an afternoon's walk or organising a family barbecue.

Like everyone else, the Queen also looks forward to her summer holiday, which is spent at Balmoral in August and September. Every year since she was a child she has ridden over the soft rolling hills surrounding the Castle, returning to favourite paths and viewpoints, and finding the peace and privacy that help to recharge her spirits.

Following the Christmas celebrations at Windsor the family take the train to Sandringham and the keen, sweeping air of Norfolk where the men go shooting and the ladies gather round the oak-log fires.

Both Balmoral and Sandringham estates are run strictly on business lines but the weeks spent at either place are probably the most idyllic part of the Royal Family's year.

Above: This photograph of Prince Philip and Princess Anne preparing a barbecue at Balmoral was taken during the making of the film, The Royal Family, in 1968
Below: In the woods at Sandringham the whole family can relax and enjoy the simple pleasure of making a bonfire

The State Coaches

Ivory Mounted Phaeton . . . Single Brougham . . . Bow-fronted Clarence . . . these are just three of the colourful names given to the thirty or so state carriages and coaches that are kept in the Royal Mews behind Buckingham Palace.

For centuries the name "Mews" was used for the place where the Royal falcons were kept during their mewing, or change of plumage. Then, when fire destroyed his stables in Bloomsbury, and Henry VIII moved his horses to the Mews near Charing Cross, the falcons were moved out—but the name Mews stayed.

Today's Royal Mews were built in 1825. As well as housing the coaches there are stables for the magnificent Windsor Greys and the Cleveland Bay carriage horses, which Prince Philip sometimes drives at the Royal Windsor Horse Show.

Almost hidden among the grand and ornate examples of coachwork is a miniature barouche—with a box for the coachman and place for a footman—which was a Christmas present to Queen Victoria's children from the Dowager Queen Adelaide in 1846. "After lunch," Queen Victoria wrote in her journal, "the three girls seated themselves inside, while the two boys sat, the one on the box, and the other standing up behind, the gentlemen dragging the carriage up and down the corridor to their intense joy."

The coach was rediscovered 15 years ago, when it was renovated and sent to Windsor so that the royal children could use it.

Another unusual item in the collection is the very handsome State Sledge which Prince Albert designed for his wife—though naturally he had to make sure it worked. At Brighton, in her diary of February 11, 1845, Queen Victoria noted that it had been snowing all the previous night, adding: "Albert tried out our pretty, smart sledge, which made him rather late for lunch."

1. The Irish State Coach, originally built by a Lord Mayor of Dublin, which the Queen normally uses for the State Opening of Parliament. Here, in 1967, Princess Anne attends for the first time
2. On the way to Princess Margaret's wedding the Queen rides in Queen Alexandra's State Coach, which is sometimes used to bring new ambassadors to Buckingham Palace to present their credentials
3. The Glass Coach, bought for King George V's coronation in 1911, has been used for nearly all the royal weddings since then. It gets its name from its large windows
4. The Scottish State Coach, not used since 1920, was restored by the St. Cuthbert's Co-operative Society for the Queen's visit to Scotland in 1969
5. The 1902 State Postillian Landau, used in 1962 for the visit of King Olav of Norway
6. A barouche with a pair of Windsor Greys. The coachmen are wearing what is called Semi-State Livery
7. A State Landau with a pair of pure-bred Cleveland Bays
8. Royal Coachmen, wearing the four distinct kinds of livery used on formal and less formal occasions
9. Royal Postillions. For the annual procession at Ascot they wear livery in the Queen's racing colours of purple, scarlet, and gold (far left)
10. The Gold State Coach which has been used for every coronation since George IV's time. Drawn by eight postillion horses, it is the only state coach that can't be used at the trot, because there's no driver's box

6

7

8

9

10

God bless the Prince of Wales

One of Prince Charles's most vivid recollections of his investiture as Prince of Wales is of accidentally sitting on his speech and having to wriggle the notes from under him in full view of television cameras and an audience of millions.

Eight years after the event opinions differ as to whether the ceremony at Caernarvon Castle in July 1969 was suggested mainly as a boost to tourism, a political expediency, or a re-enactment of meaningful pageantry. Probably it was a combination of all three. And, as with nearly all costly pieces of royal pageantry, most people—including the main participants—seem to have enjoyed themselves and thought it all worthwhile.

Prince Charles is the 21st Prince of Wales, but the ceremony of investiture had taken place at Caernarvon only once before. That was in 1911 when Charles' great-uncle, the late Duke of Windsor, was invested by his father King George V.

At the time, Prince Edward was a youth of only 17, whereas Prince Charles was nearly 21 when his turn came. And for this earlier

The simple but effective setting for the Investiture was designed by a team led by Lord Snowdon, the Castle's Constable since 1963. The total cost of organising the ceremony was £252,000.
The first-ever Prince of Wales, later to become Edward II, was born at Caernarvon Castle in 1284

investiture the young Edward was required to wear clothes that he loathed. "When a tailor appeared to measure me for a fantastic costume designed for the occasion," the Duke wrote in his autobiography, "consisting of white satin breeches, a mantle and a surcoat of purple edged with ermine, I decided that things had gone too far . . . What would my Navy friends say if they saw me in this preposterous rig?"

Prince Charles took no such risks. He wore his ceremonial uniform as Colonel-in-Chief of the Royal Regiment of Wales. But he had to face a serious threat of another kind—from militant Welsh nationalists. Leading up to the investiture there were 14 bombings altogether, including an explosion on the day itself. There was a massive security operation, and though the Queen never showed sign of it in public she must have been considerably concerned for the safety of her son.

In the end all passed off smoothly. Even the mockers must have been impressed by the sheer gallantry of it all, and by the moment—which was especially moving to most people—when the Queen placed the coronet on her son's head and straightened the purple cloak around his shoulders.

Kneeling before his Monarch and placing his hands between hers, the Prince pledged his loyalty: "I, Charles Prince of Wales, do become your liege man of life and limb and of earthly worship, and faith and truth I will bear unto you to live and die against all manner of folks."

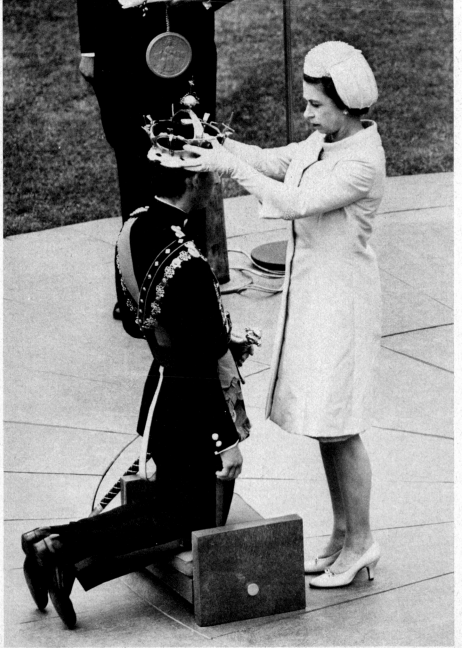

Above: *The newly-invested Prince of Wales makes his speech in the Welsh language which he learned at the University College of Wales, Aberystwyth. He went there for a term, during his course at Trinity College, Cambridge, where he studied archaeology and anthropology*

Left: *Prince Charles kneels before Her Majesty the Queen and she places on his head the coronet of the Prince of Wales. The simple design of the stool, made of blocks of slate, was the work of Lord Snowdon and his team of designers*

Below: *Prince Charles places his hands in the hands of his mother, the Queen, and she kisses him. It was one of the most moving moments in the whole ceremony of investiture, seen and remembered by the millions who watched it on television*

Right: *At the end of the ceremony the Queen leads her son to Queen Eleanor's Gate and, raising his hand, presents him to the people of his Principality*

The formal picture of Prince Charles in the robes he wore for his investiture as Prince of Wales in 1969

Right: The late Duke of Windsor, at the age of 17, when he was invested as Prince of Wales at Caernarvon Castle in 1911

Royal dogs

Around 4.30 each day the Queen is brought a tray of dishes and bowls containing cooked meat, dog biscuits and gravy. A plastic sheet is laid on the floor and, as the corgis scamper around her feet, their mistress shares out their food. It is a well-established practice which the Queen likes to take care of personally when she can.

The Queen's love of dogs, in particular corgis, seemingly dates back to her childhood when she saw the Marquess of Bath—Viscount Weymouth as he was then—playing with a corgi. She asked if she might have one too, and Dookie, the first of the royal corgis, arrived a few days later. Another, Lady Jane, had Christmas Eve puppies—Crackers and Carol—but sadly she later met with an untimely end, run over by an estate employee's vehicle.

Most of today's royal run-around of corgis are descended from Susan, who was held in such affection that she accompanied the Queen and the Duke of Edinburgh on their honeymoon. Susan was mated with an international champion of the time—Rozavel Lucky Strike—and of the ensuing pups, Sugar was kept by the Queen and Honey went to the Queen Mother. In turn, Sugar's puppies became pets of the Queen's elder children.

Susan, who was not always sweet-tempered—she was accused of nipping a sentry and a royal clock-winder—died in 1957, aged 10. Today the senior corgi is 14-year-old Heather, who is missing a hind leg

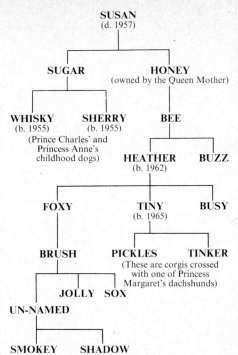

```
                    SUSAN
                   (d. 1957)
            ┌──────────┴──────────┐
         SUGAR                  HONEY
                          (owned by the Queen Mother)
    ┌───────┴───────┐            │
 WHISKY         SHERRY          BEE
 (b. 1955)     (b. 1955)    ┌────┴────┐
          (Prince Charles' and    HEATHER      BUZZ
          Princess Anne's        (b. 1962)
          childhood dogs)    ┌──────┼──────┐
      FOXY              TINY              BUSY
                      (b. 1965)
       │          ┌──────┴──────┐
     BRUSH     PICKLES        TINKER
       │       (These are corgis crossed
   ┌───┴───┐    with one of Princess
 JOLLY   SOX    Margaret's dachshunds)
   │
UN-NAMED
 ┌──┴──┐
SMOKEY  SHADOW
```

as the result of a skirmish with other Palace dogs. Pickles and Tinker are long-haired, due to a meeting between Princess Margaret's dachshund, Pipkin, and the Queen's corgi, Tiny. Jolly and Sox belong to Prince Andrew and Prince Edward.

But corgis are not the Queen's only dogs. She also breeds Labradors—a species which Prince Charles, for one, is said to prefer.

A country wedding

The wedding of Prince Richard of Gloucester, as he was then, and Birgitte van Deurs, the daughter of a Danish lawyer, had none of the pomp and less of the publicity than any other recent royal wedding. For a start, the ceremony—on July 8, 1972—took place not in a great abbey but in the tiny 13th century village church near Barnwell Manor, the ancestral home of the Gloucester family in Northamptonshire. It was the kind of quiet, simple affair that both bride and bridegroom had requested—"a compromise between the traditional English wedding and the Danish one which is smaller, jollier and more intimate", said the bride.

Birgitte, intelligent-looking with shoulder-length blonde hair, was a 20-year-old student at the Cambridge Language School when she met her future husband at a tea party. He was an undergraduate studying architecture. Both of them were light-hearted but shy people who found it easy and relaxing to be in one another's company. Prince Richard shied away from crowds and the fast world of cars and racing that his elder brother, Prince William, found so stimulating.

After she'd finished her course at Cambridge, Birgitte returned to her home in Copenhagen and worked for a year with a silversmith before starting a three-year course in commerce. By the time she returned to England and took a secretarial job at the Danish Embassy in London, Prince Richard had become a fully-fledged architect and they went out together like any other couple, with no special attention given to the fact that Richard was a cousin of the Queen. As a second son he had no fortune, no great lands to inherit, and he and Birgitte

expected to have to make their own way in the world.

Their engagement was announced on February 15, 1972. The ring the Prince gave Birgitte was an unusual one of heavy silver set with a ruby.

It poured down with rain at their wedding but the weather didn't seem to dampen anyone's spirits. The Queen Mother and Princess Margaret hurried into the church under see-through umbrellas and Prince Charles, in grey morning-suit and unconventional blue, grey and white striped shirt, seemed to enjoy himself thoroughly.

The local vicar said prayers at the service, which was conducted by the Dean of Windsor, and the groom's mother, the Duchess of Gloucester, arranged the flowers in the church—not too many because Prince William, who was best man, suffered from hay-fever. In keeping with the privacy that the bride and the bridegroom wanted there were no photographs taken inside the church. But afterwards the whole village turned out in the teeming rain to cheer their Prince and take snapshots of him and his bride in her simple dress of Swiss organdie.

Tragically, less than two months after the wedding, Prince Richard's elder brother, the 30-year-old Prince William of Gloucester, was killed when his plane crashed and burst into flames only seconds after taking off. And their father, the 74-year-old Duke of Gloucester, brother of King George VI, died two years later.

Prince Richard, who had always hoped for a peaceful life away from the limelight, became the new Duke of Gloucester, inheriting all the duties and responsibilities of a senior member of the Royal Family.

Top left: *Princess Margaret arriving at the church with Prince Charles*
Top right: *A police umbrella for the bride on arrival at the tiny village church*
Above: *The Queen Mother with the Duchess of Gloucester, the bridegroom's mother*
Below: *Prince Michael of Kent escorts Princess Alice, Countess of Athlone*
Right: *The bride and groom leaving the church*

A Royal Family album

Like most people, the Queen and Prince Philip treasure their family photographs. Nothing else shows so well how babies have grown into children, and children into adults. Photographs, especially those taken during carefree holidays, provide hours of pleasure and amusement.

In Queen Victoria's time, and right up until the reign of George VI, personal letters and diaries related the day-to-day life of members of the Royal Family—and, incidentally, provided later historians with a unique insight into events of the time. Speaking into a tape recorder and using a camera are the modern equivalents, and it will be interesting to see whether future royal biographers will have access to this kind of material in the same way as they can now study the revealing correspondence of, say, Queen Victoria.

All the members of the Royal Family are keen amateur photographers—the Queen and Princess Anne especially. And though the pictures on these pages were taken by professional photographers, they are typical of the sort the Queen likes to keep in her own family album.

Above: *Before she became Queen, Princess Elizabeth with Prince Philip, Prince Charles and Princess Anne in the garden of their home, Clarence House. The photo was taken in 1951*
Left: *Two years later, at Balmoral*
Below: *A rare view of the Queen and her family in the grounds of Windsor Castle*
Right: *This famous study of the family in the gardens of Buckingham Palace was taken by Lord Snowdon when he was still Tony Armstrong-Jones*

Left: *A spring-time walk in 1965 with the infant Prince Edward*

Above: *The Queen with Prince Charles and Princess Anne on an outing in 1958*

Below: *This picture, taken on board Britannia, was used by the Queen as her personal Christmas card in 1969*

Above: *Hand-in-hand with Prince Edward and Prince Andrew*

Right: *Examining a model of Captain Cook's ship Endeavour, before leaving for the 1970 royal tour of Australia*

Below: *This picture of the whole family was taken in Montreal in 1976*

Above: *Brother and sister together, at Sandringham*

Below: *Prince Edward and Prince Andrew, photographed by Peter Grugeon in 1975*

Right: *One of the happiest and most informal pictures ever taken of the Royal Family. The photographer was Patrick Lichfield, the place Balmoral, and the occasion the silver wedding anniversary of the Queen and Prince Philip*

Power, Parliament and the Crown

Britain is ruled by "Her Majesty's Government". Abroad, immigration officials are requested "in the name of Her Majesty" to allow a British passport holder to travel unhindered. The army, navy and air force owe allegiance not to the Government but to the Sovereign. Yet, despite all this, the Queen holds no direct power, though she does have influence.

Sir Harold Wilson told an interviewer after he left Office: "The fact that the Queen is above politics is one of the intangible advantages of monarchy."

Seven prime ministers have served the Queen during her reign so far. Winston Churchill was the first and Harold Wilson

held office the longest. In theory the monarch can dissolve Parliament and choose a new prime minister after taking advice. But since the Conservative Party, in common with the other main parties, now elect their leader it is unlikely the Queen would go against their wishes.

The relationship between Crown and Parliament is complicated and intriguing, but is most obvious nowadays in the State Opening of Parliament—the Queen's most important constitutional duty of the year.

The origins of the ceremony go back nearly 900 years before Parliament actually existed. William the Conqueror discussed affairs of state with bishops and abbots,

(later to become the Lords Spiritual), and with earls and barons, (subsequently the Lords Temporal). The talks, or parleys, were always started by the king, and took place in the parlour of the monarch's home, eventually the Palace of Westminster. As the purpose was usually to seek ways of raising money, the knights of the shire and representatives of boroughs were invited to stand at the back of the chamber and listen to what they'd be required to do.

Today the only occasion when the House of Commons and the House of Lords come together in one chamber is when the Queen opens Parliament, in the Palace of Westminster—a palace where no monarch has lived

Far left: *The full magnificence of the House of Lords, when MPs come from the Lower Chamber to hear the Queen's speech*
Left: *The formal reading of the Queen's speech. Prince Charles and Princess Anne were accompanying the Queen to the Opening for the first time, in 1967*
Above: *Returning from the State Opening of Parliament to Buckingham Palace in the Irish State coach, November 1965*

Prime Ministers during the Queen's reign

Sir Winston Churchill
1951–55 (Cons)

Sir Anthony Eden
1955–57 (Cons)

Harold Macmillan
1957–63 (Cons)

Sir Alec Douglas-Home
1963–64 (Cons)

Sir Harold Wilson
1964–70; 1974–76 (Lab)

Edward Heath
1970–74 (Cons)

James Callaghan
1976– (Lab)

for 450 years. The only change she has made to the time-honoured ceremony is an alteration in the hour—from 11.00 to 11.30 a.m.—to lessen the snarl-ups in traffic.

Before the Queen sets out from Buckingham Palace in the Irish State Coach, Yeomen of the Guard, by tradition, search the vaults of Westminster to avoid a repetition of the Guy Fawkes episode of 1605. Then, at the royal entrance, Her Majesty is greeted by the Lord Great Chamberlain and the Earl Marshal of England, (a position held, since Charles II, by successive Dukes of Norfolk), who walk up the stairs backwards, ahead of her. In the procession are a Serjeant-at-Arms and the Pursebearer. Inside the emblazoned purse, which once held the Great Seal of England, is the type-written speech, compiled by the Prime Minister and Cabinet, which the Queen will read to both assembled Houses. It sets out the Government's proposals for the coming session.

After putting on her robes and the magnificent Imperial State Crown, (weighing nearly three pounds and brought from the Tower of London for the occasion), the Queen, attended by pages and members of the Royal Family, enters the House of Lords. Only then is the House of Commons summoned. Led by the Prime Minister, the leaders of the Opposition, and the Speaker, the MPs throng to the bar—or dividing line—of the Upper House.

As soon as the Queen has delivered her speech she and the other members of the Royal Family leave the Chamber, the MPs return to the House of Commons, and the year of debating and decision-making begins. And though Parliament governs the country, only the Queen, by her Royal Assent, can technically make a bill an Act of Law.

Recent royal tours

Above: *On board the royal yacht Britannia, during last year's state visit to Finland*
Below: *On their visit to Borneo in 1972, the Queen, Prince Philip and Princess Anne toured the city of Bandar Seri Begawan, the capital of Brunei, in a magnificent chariot drawn by 40 men*

Contrary to what many people imagine, the Queen has travelled more miles abroad during the past 10 years than in the whole of the first 14 years of her reign. Since 1967 she has been to Canada five times, to Australia three times and to New Zealand twice. The total mileage covered up till February this year was over 263,000 miles.

Royal tours fall into three categories: to Commonwealth countries which recognise Elizabeth II as their Queen; to Commonwealth countries which are republics; and state visits to countries approved by the Government.

Naturally, large countries in the first category—such as Canada, Australia and New Zealand—receive the most visits, but they are usually only part of a tour that takes in a whole range of more remote places such as New Hebrides and Papua New Guinea which the Queen last visited in 1974. Government policy decrees there are some countries the Queen has so far never been to—Russia and Spain, for example—and she has not visited South Africa, which used to be such an important member of the Commonwealth, since she was a Princess.

Any royal visit abroad takes about a year to organise and involves intricate planning, even down to the smallest detail such as arranging for clothes to be dry-cleaned en route. Very often the Queen takes on holiday to Balmoral or Sandringham a whole pile of books about the background of the countries she is to visit during the following months. Then there is the question of what clothes she will wear on the tour. Hours are taken up with fittings and with discussing designs and materials. The emblem or national flower of the country she is visiting will often be worked into the material of the gown she ▶

intends wearing to the state banquet. Close attention is paid to climate and season, to tradition, and to the gifts she will take to present to her hosts.

Usually about 30 people accompany the Queen and Prince Philip on their longer tours abroad—a fraction of the number who used to surround Edward VII or George V on their travels. In addition to the Queen's private secretary, an assistant private secretary, her press secretary, two ladies-in-waiting and an equerry, the party will probably include her dresser, half-a-dozen footmen, two maids, the Queen's hairdresser, and one or two detectives. Prince Philip will usually be accompanied by his private secretary, an equerry and a valet.

State visits generally last three days and follow a pattern; a processional drive through the capital city, a visit of homage to a national cemetery or memorial, a state banquet, and attendance at a specially organised display or concert. This was the pattern of programme followed when the Queen visited Japan in 1975—she was the first reigning British monarch to do so, incidentally.

Tours of the Commonwealth countries are usually longer and less formal. Indeed the Queen introduced a completely new look to royal visits when, in Australia in 1970, she started what have become known as "royal walkabouts"—stopping the car, apparently at unplanned moments, and getting out to walk among well-wishers and chat with them about almost anything.

Even though royal visits abroad do tend to take place in autumn or winter, when most people would be glad to get away from Britain's weather, they are by no means a holiday—as Prince Philip once somewhat testily reminded Canadians: "We don't come here for our health." They involve walking through miles of class-rooms and factories.

Frequently the Queen arrives back in London after a lengthy tour looking noticeably thinner and sometimes very tired. But, with her quick eye, her sense of humour and her genuine interest in human nature there is little doubt she enjoys most of the foreign travelling she does. More important to her and her advisers is that the Sovereign should visit as many countries as possible, especially Commonwealth countries, in order to keep Britain's old friendships alive and make new friendships more possible.

Above left: *Walking through the streets of Arles, Provence, during the state visit to France in 1972*
Above: *The procession through Salvador, Brazil, in 1968*
Left: *A royal "walkabout" in Melbourne, Australia, in 1970*
Below: *A greeting for Prince Philip arriving at Kuching, Sarawak, in 1972 with the Queen and Princess Anne*

Opposite—**Top:** *Princess Anne, Prince Philip and the Queen enjoy an Eskimo display in Canada's North-West Territories*
Bottom left: *The Queen puts on slippers before entering a house in Tokyo during her state visit to Japan in 1975*
Bottom right: *Homage and presentation to the Queen during her 1974 visit to New Zealand*

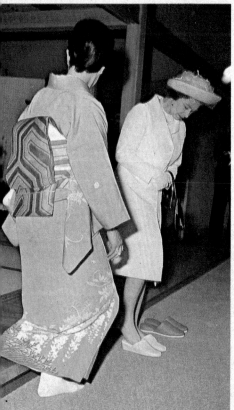

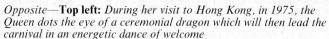

*Opposite—***Top left:** *During her visit to Hong Kong, in 1975, the Queen dots the eye of a ceremonial dragon which will then lead the carnival in an energetic dance of welcome*
Bottom left: *A petition about land rights is presented to the Queen by a group of Indians in Canada, 1976*
Bottom right: *Wandering through a busy market in Hong Kong*

Above: *In Yugoslavia, in 1972—the first state visit of a British monarch to any communist country—the Queen placed a wreath on the tomb of the unknown warrior on Mount Avala near Belgrade*
Right: *President Pompidou welcomes the Queen to Paris in 1972*
Below: *In Cooktown, Australia, Torres Strait Islanders danced in the Queen's honour, in April 1970*

Off-guard moments

Considering the millions of times the Royal Family have been photographed there are surprisingly few occasions when they have been "caught off-guard".

When official photographs are taken the Queen likes to "vet" the pictures before publication. But she has no control over news pictures, and editors are always looking for the picture that shows a member of the Royal Family in a way that is new.

Years of experience have taught the Queen, a naturally shy person, how to cope with a wall of camera-men popping off flash bulbs in her face. She is genuinely sympathetic to their work and, on royal tours, she is quick to notice if one of the regular photographers is missing or having technical difficulties.

The Queen Mother is particularly popular with press photographers. As she steps out of her car she will often pause for a moment, looking to one side then the other. And perhaps she will give a little wave or put a hand up to a shoulder, just so that each photographer has a fair chance of getting an individual shot.

Catching the Royal Family off-guard is usually easiest when they feel they are off-duty. But just now and then, even on official occasions, the camera captures a moment that provides a good chuckle for everyone, themselves included!

Princess Anne's wedding

Like her mother, Princess Anne was married in November. The day she chose, the 14th, was also her elder brother's 25th birthday. It turned out there was even another coincidence—it was the birthday of the man who performed the ceremony, Dr. Michael Ramsey, then Archbishop of Canterbury.

Less than a hundred years ago the betrothal of a sovereign's daughter would have been a private arrangement with wide political implications. The peace of nations depended to a great extent on the inter-marriage of the royal families of Europe. But in 1973 the Queen's only daughter married the man she had fallen in love with, a handsome officer in the Queen's Dragoon Guards, Captain Mark Phillips. Millions were witness to the event through television, and, apart from the Queen, the only reigning head of state at the wedding was Prince Rainier of Monaco.

Anne and Mark had first met five years before, at a party in a London cellar after the 1968 Olympic Games. The Queen Mother had taken her grand-daughter along to meet some of the top names in the world of show-jumping. "She thought I might find it rather fun," Princess Anne said later, "and I, as a beginner at eventing, was very overawed by the occasion."

Both the Princess and Mark Phillips, who grew up on a farm, have been keenly interested in horses since childhood, so during the next few years they frequently met up at horse trials and dinner parties of mutual friends. Both of them kept insisting, to each other and the world at large, that they weren't at all interested in getting married. But when the official announcement of their engagement came in May 1973 it transpired they had been unofficially engaged for some weeks already. Anne showed off her engagement ring to newsmen —a sapphire with a diamond either side— commenting: "It's pretty simple, it's beautiful," while Mark, back with his regiment in Germany, fended off pressmen's questions with characteristic simplicity: "I just love everything about her."

They had wished for a simple wedding, but

it was not to be. Anne did insist, however, that she would have just one bridesmaid—her cousin Lady Sarah Armstrong-Jones—and one page, her brother, Prince Edward.

Two days before the wedding, instead of a reception for visiting royalty like the one which had preceded their own wedding, the Queen and Prince Philip gave a dance for the young friends of Anne and Mark in the gold and crimson ballroom at Buckingham Palace. Anne, looking particularly beautiful in yellow silk, opened the dancing with her fiancé to the tune "The Loveliest Night of the Year".

The weather on the wedding day itself was crisp and clear. Thousands of well-wishers lined the route to watch the Princess set out for Westminster Abbey with her father in the wide-windowed Glass Coach that the Queen and Prince Philip had used on their wedding day to return to the Palace.

The bride was wearing a dress that was high at the neck, pin-tucked to show off her tiny waist, and with huge trumpet sleeves. Her long veil was held in place by a tiara loaned by the Queen Mother and worn by the Queen at her wedding 26 years earlier. In her bouquet of white roses and lily of the valley was a sprig of myrtle grown from Queen Victoria's wedding flowers.

It was very much a public wedding, seen by hundreds of millions of people around the world. Yet it still retained a family feeling, a case of the only daughter among four children leaving home to get married.

After the signing of the registers, and the deep curtsy of Princess Anne to the Queen, Captain and Mrs. Mark Phillips almost cantered down the aisle to the sound of the bridegroom's regimental march, all tension gone, the solemn part over.

At the wedding breakfast a television camera inside Buckingham Palace showed the bride and groom as they stepped out on to the balcony to wave to the crowds, and millions heard Princess Anne's firm aside to someone to "get off my dress".

The honeymoon began in Thatched House Lodge, a beautiful home set in a royal park within 10 miles of the Palace. It had been loaned by Princess Alexandra and her husband.

The next day the young couple flew to Barbados to join Britannia for a three-week Caribbean cruise while in wintry London thousands happily queued for hours to file past a display of their wedding presents at St. James's Palace. Among the gifts, very sensibly, were eight dozen coat-hangers from Princess Margaretha of Sweden . . .

Above: *Almost a fairy-tale picture of a Princess and her Captain of Dragoons. Princess Anne's wedding-dress went on display afterwards at St. James's Palace, along with the hundreds of wedding presents*

Below: *The formal wedding group photograph*

Cyphers Royal and Royal Standards

Left: Constantine's Labarum, the first Christian monogram.
Right: A cypher of Alfred the Great

Other versions of the cypher of William and Mary

Edward VII

George VI

Richard II and his Queen, Anne of Bohemia

William IV

Elizabeth II

Left: Henry VIII and Anne Boleyn
Right: Elizabeth I

George V

Left: Charles I as Prince of Wales
Right: William and Mary

Victoria

Edward VIII

Royal Cyphers, or monograms, have been used for centuries to indicate the reign to which a document or coin belongs. And Henry VIII was the first to add another letter after the sovereign's own initial—in his case HK (presumably Henry King) or HR, for Henricus Rex.

Today's Royal Cypher, seen most often on pillar-boxes, is not unlike some of the patterns used by Queen Elizabeth I.

The Royal Standard signifies the presence of the Queen.

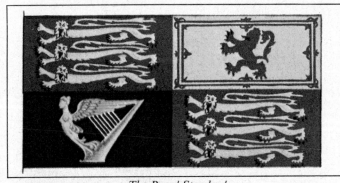

The Royal Standard

The Duke of Edinburgh's Personal Standard

The Queen Mother's Standard

The Prince of Wales' Standard

The Queen's masterpieces

The Queen's Art Collection, distributed among all the royal palaces, has been carefully built up over hundreds of years.

Henry VIII, the patron of Holbein, could be said to have laid the basis for the collection, but Charles I, who came to the Throne in 1625, was probably the most discerning royal patron of all. He employed agents all over Europe to buy works of art, and himself came back from Madrid with a number of, now priceless, Titians.

After Charles I was executed, however, Oliver Cromwell, the Lord Protector, declared all pictures confiscated. They were piled up in Somerset House, priced, then sold to collectors at home and abroad, notably to the King of Spain and Cardinal Mazarin of France. Many of the finest Raphaels and Corregios were lost to Britain for ever. But when Charles II came to the Throne he ordered everyone who had bought a painting from Cromwell to return it to the royal collection within two months, so many of the other masterpieces, at least, were restored to the royal collection.

Charles II, and later his brother James II, acquired a few more fine paintings, including Holbein's *Noli Me Tangere* at Hampton Court. Two Rubens' landscapes, now at Windsor, were collected by George II's son, Prince Frederick. George III managed to secure the wealth of Canalettos which are unrivalled in the world, besides commissioning Gainsborough to paint a series of portraits of his family. Altogether there are 34 Gainsboroughs in the Queen's Collection—the biggest single group in existence, the National Gallery having about another 20 and the Tate Gallery 14.

After Charles I, probably George IV did more than any other monarch to add to the royal collection. He knew precisely which paintings would look best in a particular kind of room, and the sort of pictures he preferred. He particularly admired Sir Joshua Reynolds' military and naval portraits and, in contrast, the sporting pictures of Stubbs and Ben Marshall. He had a passion for the Dutch and Flemish schools—which partly accounts for the number of Van Dyck, Rembrandt and Vermeer in the collection.

Queen Victoria and her husband, besides acquiring early Italian and Flemish pictures, lavishly encouraged such painters as Landseer and Winterhalter. Landseer's dramatic studies of royal animals and holidays in the Scottish Highlands had the same appeal to Queen Victoria as the Stubbs paintings of horses had to George IV.

The practice of encouraging contemporary artists has continued to the present day. Pictures by modern artists such as John Piper have been purchased by the Royal Family, and the Queen's representatives keep a watchful eye on art sales around the world.

But the Queen's greatest contribution to the enjoyment of art has almost certainly been the building of the Queen's Gallery at Buckingham Palace on the site of the private chapel which was destroyed by bombs in 1940. There is still a small chapel at one end of the Gallery, but the rest of the space is given over to public exhibitions of some of the 5,000 pictures in the Royal Collection. Since the Gallery was opened in 1962 thousands of people from Britain and all over the world have been able to see a treasure trove of pictures, many of which have never been on public view before.

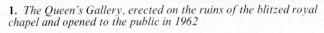

1. *The Queen's Gallery, erected on the ruins of the blitzed royal chapel and opened to the public in 1962*

2. *Study Of A Lily, a very early Leonardo da Vinci*

3. *Bruegel's Massacre Of The Innocents*

4. *Rubens' The Farm At Laeken*

5. *Elizabeth I as a princess, by an unknown artist*

6. *Stubbs' John Gascoigne With Bay Horse*

7. *The East Gallery, at the head of the Grand Staircase, in Buckingham Palace*

1. Examples of Italian art in the Queen's collection, on exhibition in 1964

2. Lady With Lap Dog by the 15th century painter Costa

3. The Adoration Of The Shepherds by the Italian painter Jacopo Bassano

4. On the left is the marble bust of King Charles I after Giovanni Lorenzo Bernini. The two larger paintings are of Burlington House, London, by Antonio Visentini and Francesco Zuccarelli, and the famous view of the Grand Canal at Venice by Canaletto. The bronze bust on the right is of Phillip II and is attributed to Leone Leoni

5. This photograph of Prince Charles in the Picture Gallery at Buckingham Palace was taken in 1969, the year of his investiture at Caernarvon

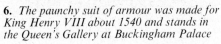

6. *The paunchy suit of armour was made for King Henry VIII about 1540 and stands in the Queen's Gallery at Buckingham Palace*

7. *Just three of the Queen's collection of paintings by the 17th century painter Van Dyck. The veneered cabinet dates from about 1665 and is one of a pair presented to King George V by Lord Rothschild*

8. *The famous painting by Van Dyck of The Five Eldest Children Of Charles I*

9. *Several artists, names unknown, may have worked on The Embarkation Of King Henry VIII for the Field Of The Cloth Of Gold*

10. *Studies of philosophers and poets—part of a series for the fresco in the Stanza della Segantura in the Vatican, painted by Raphael between 1509 and 1511*

11. *Study Of Hands by Leonardo da Vinci, probably drawn between 1478 and 1480*

12. *Michelangelo's Fall Of Phaeton*

Hàng out the banners

When a head of state visits Britain it always seems reason enough to spread grit on the roads, erect barriers on the pavements and hang banners from poles. And if many of the crowds lining the processional route don't quite recognise the President of the South American republic, and many others arrive late at their places of work because road diversions have caused traffic chaos . . . well, it is all part of the pageantry of London, and such colourful occasions don't happen that often.

Since 1954 the number of state visits has worked out at about two a year—usually in the spring and summer when the capital is looking at its leafy best. The visiting head of state—a king, an emperor, or more often a president—generally flies into Gatwick and then takes a train to Victoria where the red carpet has been rolled out and the Queen, the Prime Minister, the Foreign Secretary and a phalanx of dignitaries are waiting to greet him. Sometimes he comes alone, sometimes with his wife or—as in the case of President Saragat of Italy's visit in 1969—with his daughter. Their visit was also unusual in that they were entertained at Windsor Castle instead of Buckingham Palace—an experiment that had not happened since King Manoel of Portugal visited Edward VII, 60 years before.

The state drive to Buckingham Palace, in open coaches from Victoria Station, brings office workers rushing out on to the pavements to see the Queen as much as the distinguished visitor whose face often is not familiar to the British. When President Giscard d'Estaing of France arrived last year, however, the story was different. All eyes were on the chic figure of the President's

Above: *Many state visits to Britain begin at London's Victoria station, where the national anthems are played before the procession through the streets. Here the visitor is King Bhumibol and Queen Sirikit of Thailand*
Above left: *During the state visit of Emperor Hirohito of Japan in 1971*
Left: *President de Gaulle of France, on his state visit to Britain in 1960*
Right: *Richard Nixon, when President of the United States, calls at Buckingham Palace*
Far right: *Driving through Hyde Park with King Faisal of Saudi Arabia in May 1967*

wife who makes good use of such occasions by wearing the creations of Paris fashion designers.

The programme of a state visit normally follows the same pattern. After a light informal lunch and an exchange of gifts at the Palace, the visiting head of state will lay a wreath at the tomb of the unknown warrior in Westminster Abbey in the afternoon, be received by the Lord Mayor of Westminster at St. James's Palace, and pay a courtesy call to the Queen Mother at Clarence House.

The climax of the day comes later with the state banquet in the ballroom of Buckingham Palace. This is a magnificent room, 123 feet long and 45 feet high – the largest of the State Apartments—which was built for Queen Victoria between 1853 and 1855. It has been repainted only twice—in 1926 and 1967—but in 1946 was given a scrub-down!

Over 150 guests, including the Prime Minister and members of the Cabinet, ambassadors, diplomats, and the most senior civil servants, are served by footmen wearing scarlet livery decorated with gold braid, scarlet plush knee breeches, pink stockings and black buckle shoes.

A selection from the Queen's magnificent collection of gold plate is displayed on the walls and sideboards, while on the tables are further examples of the country's great treasures. The glass and china used may be different at each banquet, but everything is of exquisite craftsmanship.

At the banquet in honour of President Giscard d'Estaing, for instance, the table glass was of English cut crystal, hand engraved with the cypher "EIIR" and made for the Queen's coronation. The china was Louis XVth's Sevres Service in turquoise blue with a design of birds. The large groups of flowers in the corners of the ballroom were of lemon and flame gladioli.

The meal itself usually consists of four courses, with a suitable wine for each course, and is served with faultless timing. Careful instruction has been taken months beforehand about what the distinguished guest likes and doesn't like.

On the second day of the visit the foreign head of state gives a banquet in return—sometimes at his country's embassy or at a hotel. When King Faisal of Saudi Arabia came to Britain in 1967 he commissioned a designer to transform the ballroom of London's Dorchester Hotel into an oriental paradise of graceful arabesque arches, canopies, ostrich plumes and lavish gold embroidery.

But state visits are by no means all a matter of regal processions and banquets. A call is always made on the Prime Minister, sometimes an address is made to both Houses of Parliament, and often useful diplomatic and political exchanges result.

Above left: *The Queen chatting to Pierre Trudeau, Prime Minister of Canada, on his visit to Britain*
Left: *Prince Philip rides with Madame Giscard d'Estaing, wife of the French President, at the beginning of the state visit to Britain in 1976*
Above right: *The magnificent ballroom at Buckingham Palace, before a state banquet*
Right: *The Queen and the Duke of Edinburgh arrive at the Italian Embassy in London for a banquet given by the President of Italy, Giuseppe Saragat, in 1969*
Far right: *Prince Philip escorts Queen Farah Dibah at Ascot, in 1973*

Above left: *The Queen, wearing the Grand Cross of Order of the Netherlands Lion, with Queen Juliana of the Netherlands at a state banquet at Windsor in 1972*
Above: *At Windsor, with Chancellor Brandt of West Germany, again in 1972*
Left: *The start of a state banquet for President Kekkonen of Finland at Buckingham Palace in 1969*
Below left: *The arrival of President Giscard d'Estaing of France for a state visit in 1976*
Below: *The Queen welcomes President Luis Echeverria of Mexico to Windsor Castle, at the start of his three-day state visit in April 1973*
Right: *The Danish and British Royal Families link arms to enter the state banqueting room at Windsor Castle in April 1974*

Homes, not palaces

In the minds of millions around the world, Buckingham Palace is the home of the Queen of England. And so it is. But the Palace is the official home and is owned by the nation, not by the Sovereign. Balmoral Castle and Sandringham House, on the other hand—where the Royal Family spend a total of about three months in the year—are the Queen's personal property, handed down from generation to generation.

Prince Albert bought Balmoral in 1852 after Queen Victoria's leading physician, Sir James Clark, advised her to take a lengthy holiday and recommended the bracing air of Deeside, some 100 miles north of Edinburgh. He paid £31,000 for the property, then spent another £100,000 replacing the modest house with the imposing Scottish baronial-style castle of today. And there is little doubt that Balmoral Castle is the Royal Family's favourite home. It has special memories for each one of them, very often reaching back to childhood.

As a child, the Queen spent many happy holidays at Balmoral, and it was nearby that she accepted Prince Philip's proposal of marriage. Both Prince Charles and Princess Anne have said that, given the choice, they would prefer to live in Scotland, and it is quite likely Prince Charles will buy a house north of the border after he is married.

Balmoral, with its acres upon acres of heather and woodland, its rivers and nearby lochs, is the perfect place to relax. The Queen can ride for miles each morning with little chance of meeting anyone. Prince Edward can learn to drive a car on the private roads, as his brothers did, and Prince Andrew can sail with friends, play golf on the private course, or see a film in the Castle's own cinema.

When they are at Balmoral—usually from August till October—the Royal Family live very much as Scottish lairds. They shoot and fish, and often invite friends from the south to come and stay. Much of the time, both the men and ladies wear kilts of the Royal Stuart, or Balmoral tartan, which was designed by Prince Albert and combines black, red, grey and lavender.

A piper parades outside the Castle walls each morning, and three pipers play at the royal table over dinner.

On Sunday mornings the whole family joins the local people at divine service at the tiny Crathie kirk, and when the Highland Games take place at Braemar everyone goes

Balmoral Castle

Windsor Castle

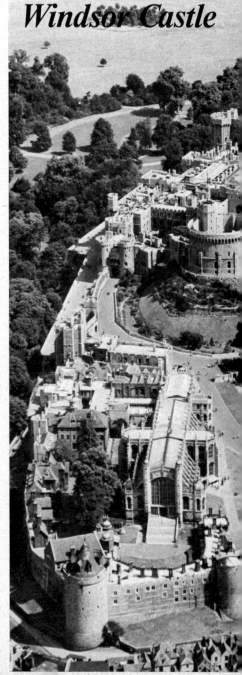

along, as they have done for years. Balmoral is very much a home for family and friends.

Sandringham, the Queen's other private home, stands in 20,000 acres on the flat, windswept coastal edge of Norfolk, about 110 miles north-east of London. It was acquired for the Prince of Wales, later Edward VII, in 1861, at a cost of £220,000 and, like Balmoral, was completely rebuilt.

Like Balmoral again, Sandringham holds a host of memories for the Queen—though not all of them happy. Her grandfather, George V, who called it "the place I love better than anywhere in the world", died there in 1936. So, too, did her father, George VI, who passed away in his sleep in February 1952.

For many years the Royal Family stayed at Sandringham over Christmas. And, like her grandfather, the Queen made her first Christmas Day broadcast from there in 1952. But more recently, Christmas has been spent at Windsor, the family going to the Sandringham estate afterwards to spend the New Year.

Though Windsor Castle cannot be counted among the personal properties of the Queen, it has become a fairly regular weekend home for herself and Prince Philip, despite the noise of aircraft flying in and out of London Airport.

Steeped in history—William the Conqueror was its first occupant—with walls as thick as the width of a normal-sized room, it looks every inch a castle. Yet the private apartments are bright and cheery, with the most modern form of central heating installed and stereo equipment cleverly designed inside antique furniture.

The Castle is probably at its liveliest at Christmas—when the whole Royal Family and staff join together in the festivities—and during Royal Ascot, in the summer, when the Queen moves to the Castle for a week and invites relatives and race-going friends to a house-party.

Here, as at Balmoral (where she stays just a few minutes away at Birkhall), the Queen Mother is always near her family. At Windsor she lives at Royal Lodge in the Great Park.

Balmoral Castle . . . Windsor Castle . . . Sandringham House. They are not palaces in the strict sense of the word, but they are certainly family homes.

Sandringham House

Heir to the Throne

Above: *One of the most charming informal pictures ever taken of Prince Charles—playing with his cousin Lady Sarah Armstrong-Jones, at Balmoral*

Below: *In 1974 Prince Charles flew in by helicopter to meet the people of Wales*

When he reached his 28th birthday last November, Prince Charles was not only the most eligible bachelor in the world, he had also become possibly the most popular heir to the Throne Britain has known. In recent times only his great-uncle, the late Duke of Windsor, has commanded comparable admiration as a young man among people of all ages and from all types of background.

However, the reasons for Prince Charles' popularity, among his own generation in particular, appear at first difficult to explain. At a time when it was fashionable to wear long hair and dress sloppily, he kept his hair trim and wore slightly out-of-date suits. As a member of the "permissive generation" he came out firmly as a believer in marriage and the family way of life. He didn't particularly want a women's liberationist as a friend, and he didn't have a cynical view of Britain's future role in the world. In other words, in the eyes and terminology of many of his own generation he was a "square". And, confronted with the description, as he was in an interview in 1975, he admitted: "All right, I've no worries, I *am* pretty square." But he went on to explain why the description didn't worry him. "So far as I'm concerned I'm going to go on believing to a certain extent things which I consider to be true and right, and decent and honourable, and if everyone changes their minds they can." In his view: "I may be square today, but I may not be in 10 years time."

Prince Charles' forthrightness, reminiscent of his father, is a characteristic that appeals to many people—not least to young people. Another is his willingness to tackle adventures which the majority of men would find too daunting. During his tour of Canada in 1975 he dived for half an hour below the 5 ft. Arctic ice, wearing a special heated rubber suit. At the age of 21 he gained a private pilot's licence, and later became the first heir apparent to make a parachute jump. The fact that he attempts hair-raising feats partly "because I'm feeling that I have to justify myself, my existence," only serves

to increase the admiration of the more faint-hearted. But he cheerfully admits there is one sport he would not like to attempt—and that's rock-climbing.

Although he is a very sensitive person, the Prince of Wales, along with most members of the Royal Family, does not have a reputation of being an intellectual, or even of having more than a passing interest in the Arts. His cello playing, which he started at Gordonstoun, suffers from lack of practice, and even though he still enjoys music very much, he seldom attends concerts. History greatly interests him; and, as he is a participant, that might be expected. He believes the whole of life is based on what has gone before, that history enables us to interpret the present and the future. Much has been written about his admiration of his forbear—George III—and what is significant are the elements in the King which he particularly admires: an ability to get on with people and a good sense of humour.

People who know him would say Prince Charles is blessed with both attributes. His sense of humour shows itself in his mimicry—he is still a great fan of the Goons—and in the laconic touch he introduces at the beginning of many of his speeches. When he spoke in the House of Lords in 1974—the first member of the Royal Family to do so for about 100 years—he chose the subject of sport and leisure and immediately won the sympathy of Their Lordships by saying: "The fact that I am making with some trepidation my maiden speech must indicate that we have a problem over recreation . . ."

Though he has now left the Royal Navy after commanding the mine-hunter Bronnington for nearly a year, Prince Charles is likely—once more, in common with his father—to retain the breezy image of the sailor. On his own admission he has "fallen in love with all sorts of girls" and his approach to life generally is positive and optimistic. His wife is unlikely to experience many dull moments.

As for the future, it will almost certainly be

many years before Charles becomes King. He does not favour abdication and he believes there are many roles he could usefully undertake apart from that of monarch. This year, much of his time will be taken up with the Queen's Silver Jubilee Appeal—encouraging young people to give service. And next year—who knows? The Prince of Wales, while having a great respect for tradition, also has a penchant for springing surprises.

Above left: *Arriving for the Royal Tournament in 1970*

Above: *Following his election as an Elder Brother of Trinity House in 1974*

Below: *Prince Charles chauffeurs Davina Sheffield, one of several girls he has escorted*

Far left: *Prince Charles, President of the British Sub-Aqua Club, under the Arctic ice where the temperature was 28·5 degrees F*

Left: *As skipper of the Bronington, Prince Charles checks to see all is clear as the ship leaves Rosyth*

Above: *Prince Charles with the Queen and Crown Equerry Lt. Colonel Sir John Miller at a polo final—for the Queen's Cup—at Smith's Lawn, Windsor, in June 1975*

Left: *Looking his most elegant, Prince Charles in topper and tails at Ascot: and arriving at London Airport on his way back to Nova Scotia in July 1975 to resume his naval duties. He had flown to London a few days previously sporting a full beard and moustache, had shaved off the beard for the Order of the Bath ceremony at Westminster Abbey, then removed the moustache—Navy regulations do not permit them*

To set before a Queen

At the age of 25 the Queen weighed 11 stones. Now, 25 years later, her weight is just over 8 stones and she has a figure that is the envy of many women. The reason is that after the birth of Princess Anne, her doctors advised her to take regular exercise and to keep to a fairly strict diet—and she has done so ever since.

According to friends, Her Majesty still has a weakness for peppermint creams and chocolate cake, but the hearty appetite which she displayed as a young woman has either diminished, or been controlled.

For breakfast the Queen usually has an egg dish, or sometimes kippers or kidneys, followed by toast spread with butter, marmalade or honey. She takes milk with her tea, but no sugar.

The main course at lunch may be fish or lean meat, accompanied by one or two potatoes and fresh vegetables from the kitchen gardens at Windsor. Generally there is a side salad which is dressed with oil and vinegar.

The Queen eats, and drinks, sparingly. Before dinner she may have a Martini or a sherry followed, perhaps, by a glass of sparkling hock with her meal. But, as those sitting near her at banquets have discovered, the Queen can sip at a glass all evening while others are savouring several vintages. From long experience she also knows how to work her way through a sumptuous menu without eating too much.

When she travels abroad her hosts are made aware of her preferences—and that she avoids raw fish and doesn't care for caviare—but there are occasions when good manners prevent her from taking any avoiding action. During her visit to Japan in 1975 the Queen was invited to sample a cup of the traditional green tea. Her hosts, smiling, watched their guest sip from the small cup and waited for her to comment on the drink. The Queen replied with one word: "Surprising".

Buckingham Palace does not disclose the Queen's precise diet, preferring simply to say that she eats sparingly and takes a great deal of exercise. So these representational pictures show the kind of fare that is set before the Royal Family.
The photograph on the left was taken at a traditional tea ceremony during the Queen and Prince Philip's visit to Japan in 1975

The whole family gathered for the Silver Wedding celebrations. **1** The Earl of Snowdon; **2** The Duke of Kent; **3** Prince Michael of Kent; **4** The Duke of Edinburgh; **5** The Earl of St. Andrews, (elder son of the Duke of Kent); **6** Prince Charles; **7** Prince Andrew; **8** Hon. Angus Ogilvy and, **9**, his son, James Ogilvy; **10** Princess Margaret; **11** The Duchess of Kent (holding Lord Nicholas Windsor, her younger son); **12** The Queen Mother; **13** The Queen; **14** Princess Anne; **15** Marina Ogilvy and Princess Alexandra; **16** Lady Sarah Armstrong-Jones; **17** Viscount Linley; **18** Prince Edward; **19** Lady Helen Windsor, (daughter of the Duke of Kent)

Silver wedding bells

Celebrating her silver wedding anniversary five years ago, the Queen summed up her feelings like this: "A marriage begins by joining man and wife together, but this relationship between two people, however deep at the time, needs to develop and mature with the passing years. For that it must be held firm in the web of the family relationships, between parents and children, between grandparents and grandchildren, between cousins, aunts and uncles.

"If I am asked today what I think about family life after 25 years of marriage I can answer with simplicity and conviction. I am for it."

The Queen was speaking at a luncheon in her honour at London's Guildhall. Sitting at the top table, she and the Duke of Edinburgh looked almost as young as they did on their wedding day. Before the lunch they attended a simple thanksgiving service at Westminster Abbey to celebrate the occasion and thoughtfully asked nearly 100 couples

Left: *The procession into Guildhall at the City of London's lunch in honour of the Queen and Prince Philip's silver wedding*
Below left: *Setting out for the lunch at Guildhall from Buckingham Palace*
Below: *The blessing at the close of the thanksgiving service at Westminster Abbey*

married on the same day to join them. One of the husbands explained he and his bride had deliberately chosen the day of the royal wedding to get married themselves "because I thought there was a good chance I would remember our anniversary."

At the Guildhall luncheon the Queen was in as happy and relaxed a mood as anyone could remember seeing her. She told the Lord Mayor and 600 guests: "I think everybody really will concede that on this day of all days I should begin my speech with the words 'My husband and I'". Prince Philip looked up at her, smiling, as she went on: "Neither of us is much given to looking back and the years have slipped by so quickly. Now that we have reached this milestone in our lives we can see how immensely lucky we have been, or perhaps fortunate might be a better word.

"We had the good fortune to grow up in happy and united families. We have been fortunate in our children, and above all we are fortunate in being able to serve this great country and Commonwealth."

Photographs specially taken at Balmoral to mark their silver wedding show the Queen and Prince Philip as not only a very handsome but also a relaxed middle-aged couple. There are lines about their faces—without any apparent effort to disguise them—but only the lines you expect to see on the parents of a family of four, the eldest two of whom are now themselves adult.

Throughout their married life there have never been any serious rumours of a rift, though perhaps early on Prince Philip did raise a few eyebrows by spending months at a time on protracted lone tours around the world. But these were almost entirely in the course of duty, and the Queen better than anyone knows that her husband is a man who can be happy only if he is busy about something, extending his own knowledge and spurring others to greater achievements.

In character, the Queen and Prince Philip complement one another. The Queen, it is said, is quite happy with her own company—and at times grateful for a bit of peace and quiet. She is probably more patient than Prince Philip and her very strong sense of humour is more tolerant of human nature. But what they both share above all is a love of family and family life. In a sense it is what they stand for, whether it be their own family or, on a wider scale, the Commonwealth as a family of nations.

The strength of the married life of the Queen and Prince Philip is very much reflected in their children's attitude to home and their parents. Prince Charles in particular is grateful for the way he was brought up. He once paid the kind of tribute any parent would like to have. "I'm very lucky because I have very wise and terribly sensible parents who have created a marvellous, secure, happy home." He admitted he had needed discipline: "If I hadn't had it I'd have been abominably spoiled and a miserable sort of youth". And he showed himself to hold views on family life every bit as strong as his parents, when he said: "I personally believe that the family unit is the most important aspect of our particular society".

The Queen's first "walkabout" in London—when she chatted to several people at random—took place in the modern Barbican on her silver wedding anniversary in November 1972

Attendant upon the Queen

Whenever the Queen tours a hospital, visits a factory or attends a concert there is invariably another well-dressed woman following just a few steps behind. Very often people are puzzled as to who this is. In fact she is one of the Queen's ladies-in-waiting, a select band of women who—when they are with the Queen—wear a diamond brooch in the shape of the royal cypher.

Altogether there are 10 ladies-in-waiting personal friends of the Queen whom she has chosen to assist with her duties. Their main job is to attend to correspondence, take private telephone calls, make sure the Queen has her speech, or her gloves, or whatever else she may require at a particular moment during a public engagement. They are the Queen's shadows, always prepared to step forward in any minor crisis, but aware that their place is normally in the background.

Chief among them is the Duchess of Grafton who, in 1967, took over the duties of Mistress of the Robes from the Duchess of Devonshire. Normally a lady-in-waiting will attend the Queen for two weeks at a time, with an interval of six weeks in between. One of the duties of the Duchess is to organise a rota which takes account of school holidays and family commitments.

The more senior ladies-in-waiting are known by the ancient title of Ladies of the Bedchamber. They usually accompany the Queen to events such as galas and on provincial tours. At present there are three Ladies of the Bedchamber: the Marchioness of Abergavenny, who shares the Queen's love of horses and was at one time Joint Master of the Eridge Hunt; the Countess of Airlie—an American, and a sister-in-law of Angus Ogilvy; and the Countess of Cromer, the wife of a former British Ambassador to

Washington, who is officially an "extra" Lady of the Bedchamber.

In addition to the Ladies there are the Women of the Bedchamber, who have an office at Buckingham Palace and are paid a small salary for their work. Among them are Lady Susan Hussey, who at 21 was the youngest ever to be chosen by the Queen; Lady Abel Smith; and Mrs. John Dugdale, wife of the Lord Lieutenant of Salop.

It is not only the Queen who is attended by ladies-in-waiting. Senior members of the Royal Family also enjoy the comfort of having a friend by their side when they go to a function where everyone knows who they are but they may recognise no-one at all!

Right: *A lady-in-waiting helps the Queen put on her raincoat during a visit to Clydebank in 1953*
Below: *Lady Susan Hussey, one of the Queen's youngest ladies-in-waiting, welcomes the Emperor of Japan to London in 1971*
Bottom left: *Leaving for Corsica, accompanied by Lady Rose Baring*
Bottom right: *Arriving at Sandhurst to take the salute at the Sovereign's Parade in 1965*

"I am speaking to you..."

In a small room under the staircase at Sandringham, King George V made the first historic Christmas Day broadcast in 1932. "Through one of the marvels of modern science," he began, "I am enabled this Christmas Day to speak to all my peoples throughout the Empire..."

The only other time the general public had heard his voice was in 1924 when he opened the Empire Exhibition at Wembley. After King George V died in 1936 there were no more Christmas Day royal broadcasts until 1939, at the start of the second world war, when King George VI inspired hope with the simple message: "Winter lies before us, cold and dark... but after winter comes spring."

The King was nervous of speaking into a microphone. "This is always an ordeal for me and I don't begin to enjoy Christmas until after it is over," he once confided. And at first the Queen also felt apprehensive, although over the years all trace of nervousness seems to have disappeared.

She made her first Christmas broadcast as Queen from Sandringham, live, in 1952: "As my beloved father used to do, I am speaking to you from my own home, where I am spending Christmas with my family; and let me say at once how I hope that your children are enjoying themselves as much as mine are on a day which is especially the children's festival, kept in honour of the Child born at Bethlehem."

Five years later the Queen went on television, again live, watched by her own family and millions of others. "It's inevitable," she said, "that I should seem a rather remote figure to many of you. A successor to the kings and queens of history; someone whose face may be familiar in newspapers and films but who never really touches your personal lives. But now at least for a few minutes I welcome you to the peace of my own home."

The friendly intimacy of the Queen's broadcasts have become such an integral part of many people's Christmas Day that there was disappointment when the Queen decided not to televise a message in 1969. The film Royal Family having been shown four times in 12 months, it was mistakenly judged that another royal broadcast might prove too much of a good thing.

In recent years the Queen's Christmas message, while still being delivered in a quiet tone, has increasingly contained sentiments that many see as matching—and perhaps sometimes even questioning—aspects of the times we live in. In 1975, talking about our need to make the best of ourselves, the Queen said: "We may feel powerless alone but the joint efforts of individuals can defeat the evils of our time. Together they can create a stable, free and considerate society."

Above left: *The first Christmas broadcast by King George V*
Above: *King George VI talks to the nation at the outbreak of World War II*
Left: *The Princesses Elizabeth and Margaret making their first broadcast in 1940*
Below: *Princess Elizabeth speaking from South Africa on her 21st birthday*

Left: *The Queen making her first Christmas Day broadcast after her coronation in 1953 from Government House, Auckland, New Zealand*
Below: *The most informal televised Christmas Day broadcast to date—in 1971*

Princess Anne at the Olympics

Princess Anne is a very determined person, and once she realised she had a chance of being selected for the British equestrian team to compete in the 1976 Olympic Games it became obvious she was going all out to gain that place. She trained as hard, if not harder, than anyone else. She refused to let the fact that she was the Queen's daughter be either a help or a hindrance. She wanted to be selected or rejected on her riding skill alone, and that rule was applied by her husband, Captain Mark Phillips, as well. He also had a strong chance of getting into the British team.

After months of tension and hard work, Princess Anne almost certainly earned her team place finally when she won the Silver Medal in the European Equestrian Championships at Luhmuehlen, West Germany in September 1975. The following April both the Princess and Lucinda Prior-Palmer were asked not to compete on their best horses at the Badminton trials, which made it seem practically certain their selection was merely a matter of time.

But later the same month Princess Anne was knocked unconscious when her horse fell at the Portman Horse Trials. A hospital examination revealed that she had also cracked a vertebra and several doctors forecast that it would be touch and go whether the Princess would be fully recovered in time for the Olympics.

However, as if to underline her determination, Anne was back in the saddle only three weeks later, and by June—when she competed in the Bramham Horse Trials—she showed she had lost none of her confidence and skill. The only slight question-mark still in the minds of the selectors was whether it wouldn't be a better bet to make Anne the reserve, and put her husband in the team. But after a final work-out at Osberton, Nottinghamshire, their minds were made up. The team to go to Montreal would comprise Lucinda Prior-Palmer, Richard Meade, Hugh Thomas and Princess Anne, with Mark Phillips as reserve.

Princess Anne insisted on being treated by the press and officials like any other member of the Olympic squad. She and Mark Phillips flew economy class to Canada, queued up in the Olympic village canteen along with everyone else, and lived in a three-roomed chalet. As a competitor the Princess was also entitled to £1 a day pocket money and a free bus pass.

In the grand opening parade before the Queen, Princess Anne, dressed identically to all the other British women competitors, was almost lost in the sea of hats and uniforms. Her father spotted her, but the Queen—like most of the millions of television viewers around the world—unfortunately didn't.

Princess Anne's first appearance as a competitor was in the dressage event, when her horse Goodwill finished that phase in 26th place. But disaster struck a few days later during the cross-country section of the contest when her horse slipped in the mud at the 19th fence and Princess Anne, thrown heavily to the ground, was badly concussed. She bravely remounted to finish the course, but the slip put her down to 28th place. Like many other competitors with high British hopes, the Princess returned disappointed. But whatever her feelings, nothing can take away from the fact that she was chosen to compete in the Olympics for Britain. And that happens to few enough people, let alone to a member of a Royal Family.

The Queen in America

Two days and 200 years after the Americans decided they would no longer be a British colony, the Queen stepped ashore in Philadelphia. To the disappointment of many, she and Prince Philip had not arrived in Concorde but had flown first to Bermuda in an RAF aircraft, then sailed the rest of the way in Britannia, to join Americans in their bicentennial celebrations.

The Queen's first invitation was to view the original Liberty Bell, cast in 1752 for the Assembly of the Colony of Pennsylvania, but now cracked. Then—for once outdoing the Americans in size—she presented Philadelphia with a new bell, six times the weight of the old one. Cast in the same foundry—in Whitechapel, London—as the original, this one has an electric motor to drive the hammer.

The next stop for the Queen and Prince Philip was Washington, where they arrived to the accompaniment of gun shots and police sirens. But, to the enormous relief of Secret Service agents, the shots were connected with a suspected bank robber on the loose, and not with an assassination attempt on the Queen or the President.

That night a state dinner was given by President Ford in an air-conditioned marquee erected over the entire White House rose-garden. The 24 tables were covered with specially designed silk tablecloths and centre-pieces of flowers arranged around single pink candles. The china and glass had originally been chosen for the White House by President Kennedy's wife.

The guest list of 200 included such names as Lady Bird Johnson, Alistair Cooke, Cary Grant and Merle Oberon. Bob Hope provided the cabaret afterwards and when the Queen took to the dance floor with President Ford the seal was set on an extremely successful occasion.

The Queen slept in what is appropriately called The Queen's Bedroom, in the White House. Decorated entirely in shades of rose-pink, it has a large four-poster bed with

The Queen and President Ford take the floor after the banquet at the White House during the Queen's visit to America
Below: President Ford, the Queen, Mrs. Ford and Prince Philip greet the guests before the banquet in honour of the Queen
Below right: The Queen being shown the celebrated Liberty Bell in Philadelphia

Opposite—**Top:** *The Queen visits the Lincoln memorial, with its shimmering white columns which have earned Washington the name of "wedding cake city"*
Bottom: *A welcoming crowd watches the Queen as she walks around the grounds of the University of Virginia, Charlottesville*

Above: *The Queen entertains President Ford at the British Embassy in Washington*
Above right: *A friendly wave for the gathering of students at the University of Virginia, Charlottesville*
Below: *This enormous cake—a model of the royal yacht Britannia—was designed to welcome the royal couple to Boston*

silk draperies and canopy. The dressing table is gilt, with gold candelabra at each side. The gilt overmantel was presented to President Truman by the Queen on behalf of her father when she first visited the White House.

Prince Philip had the Lincoln's Room with its enormous rosewood bed. There is some doubt about whether Abraham Lincoln did in fact sleep there, but other presidents, including Roosevelt and Woodrow Wilson, undoubtedly did.

The reciprocal dinner at the British Embassy the following evening was, if anything, an even grander affair than the White House party, with a banquet for 400 and a reception for 1,600 afterwards. And

the Embassy forfeited its usual Queen's birthday celebration party to help pay for it. This time the guests included Muhammad Ali and Elizabeth Taylor. The music was provided by pupils from the Yehudi Menuhin school in England.

From Washington the royal tour continued to New York and the traditional ticker-tape reception, and then on to Boston and a church service in the building where, in 1775, Paul Revere hung a lantern to warn that the British were approaching.

The final engagement of the tour was a reception aboard Britannia for 200 distinguished Bostonians before the royal party set out for Montreal and the 1976 Olympics.

The Queen's jewellery

Above: *The Diamond Diadem, designed by George IV, was worn by the Queen on her way to the Coronation and to subsequent State Openings of Parliament. It is often called Queen Victoria's diadem, because she wears it in some of her best-known portraits*
Left: *The priceless two-diamond brooch, cut from the famous Cullinan diamond*
Below: *A lapel brooch set with a large pink diamond from Tanganyika in the centre of a white diamond flower. It was a present from the late Dr. J. T. Williamson who owned the mine in which the diamond was found*

Above: *Affectionately known as "Granny's tiara" this was originally a gift to Queen Mary from the Girls of Great Britain and Ireland*
Right: *Either drop pearls or cabochon emeralds are usually hung in the centre of this magnificent tiara of interlaced diamonds. The cabochon emerald necklace and earrings were made for Queen Mary*

Above: *The triple string of pearls was a present from George V, the diamond bow brooch from Queen Mary*
Below: *The Russian Fringe tiara originally belonging to Queen Alexandra*
Right: *The diamond brooch was a present from Australians in 1954*

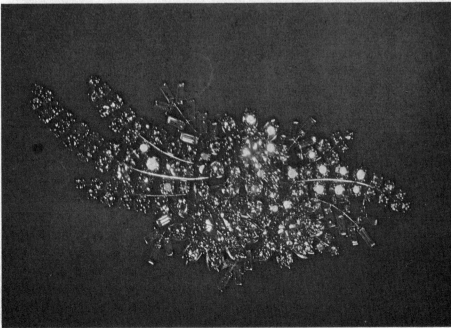

Governor of the Church

The Queen is, under God, the Supreme Governor of the Church of England. She has the duty, regulated by statute, to nominate archbishops and bishops and, on the advice of the First Lord of the Treasury, she makes other Church appointments that are, as the saying goes, "in the gift of the Crown."

But she is not just the head of the Church of England in title. She has a strong personal faith which affects her attitude to almost everything. (Though she rarely expresses her views publicly on controversial issues she did see fit last year to condemn as "obnoxious" a proposed film about the sex life of Christ.)

Wherever she is in the world the Queen makes a point of going to worship on Sunday. When she is away from home, staying the weekend with friends or relatives, she goes to the local parish church. At Windsor there is the Royal Chapel, but when she is at Balmoral the Queen attends the Church of Scotland service at Crathie. In Scotland the sovereign is not the titular head of the Church.

In her actions over the years, especially in the early part of her reign, the Queen has shown that she believes strongly in the closer relationship of all Christian churches. In 1953 she was the first to send a donation to the Presbyterian Church in Wales' appeal to build chapels and mission halls in new housing areas. The following year she became the first reigning monarch since the Reformation to contribute to a Roman Catholic cause—the rebuilding of the blitz-damaged St. George's Cathedral in South-wark, London.

During the state visit to Italy in 1961 she made her second visit to the Vatican—the first was 10 years earlier when, as Princess Elizabeth, she was received by Pope Pius XII. At the meeting with Pope John XXIII, television cameras followed her through the long corridors and ante-chambers and, dressed in black with a lace veil held in place by her Russian fringe tiara, the Queen appeared tense and nervous. But then the red damask door swung open and Pope John—all in white save for his scarlet cape—welcomed her with a warm smile and his arms outstretched. For ten minutes, behind closed doors, the Queen, Prince Philip and the Pope conversed in French. Diplomatically the Papal Throne and dais had been replaced by three damask and gold arm-chairs so that everyone was sitting at the same level under the scarlet canopy.

The audience in all lasted 26 minutes, during which the Pope presented the Queen with a set of Roman coins found in the catacombs, and a set of Papal stamps for Prince Charles and Princess Anne. Her Majesty in turn gave the Pope an ebony walking stick with a rhinoceros tusk handle and a silver framed photograph of the Royal Family. As the audience ended, the line of Swiss Guards spontaneously gave the Queen three hearty cheers.

The Queen spends Christmas, the most important event in the Christian calendar, at Windsor with as many of her family as can join her. And, like millions of others around the world, she sings carols in her church—wishing peace on earth and goodwill to all.

Far right: *The historic meeting of the Governor of the Church of England and Pope John XXIII at the Vatican in May 1961*
Above: *The Queen and her family after the Christmas Day service, 1968, at St. George's Chapel, Windsor*
Right: *Exchanging a word with her cousin, the Rev. Andrew Elphinstone, after his daughter's wedding at Worplesdon, Surrey*

Below: *The Queen addressing the second General Synod of the Church of England in 1975. On her left is the Archbishop of Canterbury, and on her right, the Archbishop of York*

Royal nights out

"In the gracious presence of Her Majesty the Queen"... With these words the organisers of events in aid of charity can be almost certain of selling every ticket in the house. But if the Queen accepted all invitations to attend premieres, she would never be able to spend an evening at home, let alone attend other functions.

In practice, the Queen and the Queen Mother take it in turn to go to the annual Royal Variety Performance, and usually the Queen also attends two film premieres in aid of charity each year.

For these functions she wears a dazzling gown, a diamond tiara, and some of her finest jewellery. For the Queen knows how much people enjoy seeing their monarch dressed in all the finery of royalty. In fact, when she goes to a premiere, it is really the stars she meets, and the audience, who feel they are having a night out.

For her own "nights out", the Queen occasionally takes a party of friends to a theatre in London's West End, dines with friends at their homes, or simply goes to the pictures—in the private cinema at the rear of Buckingham Palace.

Opposite—**Top left:** *The Queen meets Kojak (Telly Savalas) after the Royal Variety Performance of 1975*
Top right: *Arriving at the London Palladium for a "night out" in 1972*
Bottom: *Time for a joke with the cast of TV's Dad's Army, again in 1975*

Above: *Attending the premiere of the film Waterloo, in 1970*
Top right: *The Royal Variety Performance in 1965 was notable, apart from anything else, for Shirley Bassey's peep-hole dress*
Middle: *While on holiday from Benenden, Princess Anne accompanied her parents and Prince Charles to a French play at the Aldwych, London, in 1967*
Right: *Princess Anne, in black velvet cape and vivid, yellow silk gown, with the Queen— equally stunning in a dress of jade green lace —at the 1969 Royal Variety Performance*

The Queen and Prince Philip, in the library at Balmoral—this picture is one of a number specially taken to commemorate the Queen's Silver Jubilee

During the Queen's reign...

1952

Floods in Lynmouth, Devon, killed 30 people and destroyed 60 houses

1953

Edmund Hillary (above) and Sherpa Tenzing scaled Everest

1954

Roger Bannister became the first man to run a mile in under four minutes

1955

Clement Attlee, first Labour Prime Minister after the war, retired

1956

Burgess and Maclean, Foreign Office diplomats, turned up in Moscow after four years' disappearance

1957

Dr. Albert Schweitzer appealed for ban on nuclear arms and tests

1958

Cardinal Roncalli, Patriarch of Venice, was elected as Pope John XXIII at the age of 76

1959

Fidel Castro won victory in the Cuban Revolution

1960

Aneurin Bevan, hero of the British Labour Party, died of cancer

1961

Angela Mortimer won first all-British women's Wimbledon finals since 1914

1962

Marilyn Monroe died, aged 36

1963

President John Kennedy was assassinated in Dallas

1964

The Beatles triumphed on their American tour

1965

Sir Winston Churchill died

1966

The Aberfan disaster – a colliery tip engulfed a school. The final death toll was 144, including 116 children

1967

Dr. Christiaan Barnard performed first human heart transplant

1968

Senator Robert Kennedy, brother of the dead President, was assassinated in Los Angeles

1969

Armstrong and Aldrin became the first men to land on the moon

1970

Ian Smith's government proclaimed Rhodesia a republic

1971

Decimalisation, with its 50 pence piece, was introduced to Britain

1972

The Duke of Windsor died in Paris

1973

The last American soldiers left Vietnam

1974

President Nixon resigned following the Watergate disclosures

1975

Mrs. Margaret Thatcher was elected Leader of the Conservative Party

1976

Jimmy Carter was elected the 39th President of the United States